# PRACTICAL KNOWLEDGE

# PRACTICAL KNOWLEDGE

Yves R. Simon

*Edited by*
Robert J. Mulvaney

Fordham University Press
New York
1991

© Copyright 1991 by FORDHAM UNIVERSITY PRESS
All rights reserved.
LC 90-85757
ISBN 0–8232–1316–1 (clothbound)
ISBN 0–8232–1317–X (paperback)

1   3   5   7   9   10   8   6   4   2

Printed in the United States of America

# CONTENTS

| | |
|---|---|
| Editor's Note | vii |
| 1. The Ultimate Practical Judgment | 1 |
|     Practical Judgment as the Form of Action | 3 |
|     The Synthesis of Practical Judgment | 5 |
|     Nature and Use | 9 |
|     The Truth of Practical Judgment | 11 |
|     Judgment by Inclination | 17 |
|     The Incommunicability of the Ultimate Practical Judgment | 23 |
|     Fulfillment and Explanation | 26 |
| 2. On Moral Philosophy | 41 |
|     Moral Science in Socrates and Aristotle | 41 |
|     Moral Philosophy as a Theoretical Study | 47 |
|     Moral Philosophy as Intrinsically Practical | 57 |
|     Truth and Communication | 68 |
| 3. Disputed Questions | 79 |
|     The Problem of Practically Practical Science | 79 |
|     Ethics and Christian Philosophy | 87 |
|     The Timely Need for Moral Philosophy | 96 |
|     Appendix: Extracts from Correspondence of Yves R. Simon and Jacques Maritain | 100 |
| 4. From the Science of Nature to the Science of Society | 115 |
|     The Emergence of Social Science | 115 |
|     Practical Knowledge of Social Science | 120 |
|     Nature and Use in Social Science | 125 |
|     From Social Science to the Philosophy of Society | 131 |
| 5. Christian Humanism: A Way to World Order | 137 |
|     The Illusions of Social Science | 137 |

## CONTENTS

| | |
|---|---|
| The Conflict Between Humanism and Christianity | 144 |
| Humanism and Christianity: A Possible Synthesis | 148 |
| Index | 157 |

# EDITOR'S NOTE

YVES R. SIMON (1903–1961) was one of the greatest modern students of the ancient virtue of practical wisdom, called *phronesis* by Aristotle, and *prudentia* by his great Latin commentators in the Middle Ages, such as St. Thomas Aquinas. Simon's interest in this virtue ranged from ultimate theoretical concerns, such as the relationship between practical knowledge and science, to the most concrete and immediate questions of the role of practical wisdom in personal and social decision-making. These concerns, moreover, occupied Simon from the beginning of his professional life until the end. We find them in his earliest published books, such as the 1934 *Critique de la connaissance morale*. And we find them in the final correspondence with his friend and mentor Jacques Maritain, where he expresses plans to publish another book on the same set of issues. Throughout his writings practical wisdom (Simon usually uses "prudence") and its related philosophical ramifications emerge time and again in books as varied in theme as *Nature and Functions of Authority*, *Philosophy of Democratic Government*, *The Tradition of Natural Law*, *Work, Society, and Culture*, and many others. Practical knowledge, in its full richness, is a kind of pedal point to Simon's whole encyclopedic effort, recognized by him as a central unifying motif deserving his concentrated attention in the months before his untimely death.

Simon did not live to see his proposed book on practical knowledge to completion. He had already published two papers which he planned to include in his book. But, aside from some text for another chapter, he was able to finish only a draft of additional material, some notes, and a group of letters to Maritain dealing with the more crucial details of the proposed argument. What follows is an effort to reconstruct what would have been Simon's final book had he lived long enough to finish it. This brief preface is intended to present a description of its contents and organization.

## EDITOR'S NOTE

Among Simon's papers we find a series of projected studies under the general heading "Philosophical Inquiries." Volume 15 in this series is entitled "A Critique of Practical Knowledge." Its outline, in Simon's own hand, contains four chapters, three of which are given titles: "Chapter 1. On Practical Judgment"; "Chapter 2. On Moral Philosophy"; "Chapter 3. On Concrete Ethics." A "Chapter 4" is mentioned, but no title is given. That this was to be the general outline of his projected book is reinforced by a comment in a letter to Jacques Maritain, dated February 11, 1961 (three months to the day before Simon's death): "In the book of *Critique of Practical Knowledge* that I am preparing, the paper . . . 'Introduction to the Study [of Practical Wisdom]' is followed by a chapter 'On Moral Philosophy.' An old paper on 'the Science of Nature and the Science of Society' would, after revision, make up a third chapter." The general outline and contents of his proposed work seem clear. It was to begin with a treatment of the virtue of practical wisdom. This would be followed by a more theoretical account of practical knowledge and would conclude with concrete applications to issues of social philosophy and social science.

The present book is faithful to this plan. Chapter 1 consists of Simon's landmark essay on the concept of command, "Introduction to the Study of Practical Wisdom," originally published in *The New Scholasticism* (34 [1961], 1–40). It is offered here with a few corrections and some minor editorial alterations. Chapters 2 and 3 correspond to Simon's projected chapter on moral philosophy. They are taken from manuscript material some of which is virtually in final form, but most of which exists in the form of preliminary drafts and notes. It has been necessary to organize and distribute this material with considerable editorial latitude, but I have tried to be as faithful to the manuscript sources as possible. I have avoided extensive rewriting in the belief that it was more desirable to present Simon's arguments as precisely as possible, even if in unfinished prose. The reader will note the resultant difference of stylistic and rhetorical tone in these two chapters. Another practical consequence of this overall strategy was the decision not to incorporate the Simon/Maritain correspondence within the text of these chapters, but to append it to Chapter 3. Letters have an integrity of their own, and I thought it best to maintain their unity by grouping them after the relevant chapters. The appended excerpts omit only issues extraneous to the argument and material of a more personal and private nature. Chapter 4 fulfills Simon's intention to include in the book his article "From the Science of Nature to the Science of Society" originally published in *The New Scholasticism* (27 [1953], 280–304). Again some minor editorial interpolations have been made, but the chapter conforms substantially to its original. The final chapter of the book represents an editorial choice, made at the suggestion of Mrs. Paule Y. Simon, to include a paper Simon presented on the occasion of a conference to mark the seventy-fifth anniversary of Marquette University. Originally published in a commemorative volume, *From Disorder to World Order* (Milwaukee: The Marquette University Press, 1956), the piece has long been out of print. Since it represents yet another application of the general themes developed in Chapters 1–3, and given what seems to be its unusual timeliness at the present moment, we decided to round off the volume by including it.

The five chapters of *Practical Knowledge* move rhythmically from issues of immediacy and concreteness to superordinate theoretical assumptions and back again to practical applications. In Chapter 1, "The Ultimate Practical Judgment," we begin at the end, so to speak, with a consideration of the concept of "command," *imperium*, the element of practical wisdom that constitutes the form of moral action and synthesizes moral judgment with the action performed. It is practical reason as imperative that raises all the central issues treated in this book. So, for instance, command is immediately involved with the use of the material conditions of action and requires moral virtue for its full effectiveness. Deliberation requires a connaturality of mind and heart, such that the virtue of practical wisdom may alone be considered both intellectual and moral. But practical judgments at the moment they touch action are radically non-scientific and incommunicable. They fulfill the demands of virtue but cannot fully explain what they command.

Practical knowledge is chiefly practical wisdom. But it is also science and philosophy. Chapters 2 and 3 bring us to these cognate concerns. Situating his account against the background of Greek intellectualism, Simon explores the twin vocation of moral philosophy as directive (qua "moral") and theoretical (qua "philosophy"). It is *human use* which distinguishes moral philosophy from all other forms of theoretical knowledge, including psychology. Moral philosophy is a "theoretically practical science" and directs action only "at a distance." The incommunicability of prudential judgments and its allied notion of truth make the contemporary condition of moral philosophy unusually critical. Moral truth consists in conformity of action with right desire or a good will. But this is insufficient for science. Explanation is a great modern need, and the moral philosopher who wishes to maintain the classic theory of practical wisdom has huge explanatory tasks facing him.

Some controversial issues concerning Maritain's notion of "practically practical science" and the notion of Christian philosophy occupy us in Chapter 3. Simon rejects the notion of "practically practical science," insisting that by this point any viable notion of science (but especially Aristotle's) is no longer appropriate. There are moral science and directive wisdom, but no science at the moment of action itself. A useful analogy is found in another controverted topic, the notion of "Christian Philosophy." Moral theology, because of the exigencies of revelation, gives moral choice a position of certainty beyond rational attainment. But this does not mean that moral philosophy is reducible to moral theology, or that it is a species of moral theology. Moral theology does not make the judgments of moral choice more "scientific" than they are, any more than does some purported "practically practical science." Rather it may be the case that moral theology is concerned less with explanatory matters than with matters of fulfilling the demands of moral virtue. In this sense moral philosophy, while still charged with the task of explanation, may be subordinated to moral theology.

Chapter 4, "From the Science of Nature to the Science of Society," and Chapter 5, "Christian Humanism: A Way to World Order," present us with two applications of Simon's general position. The social sciences are a uniquely modern phenomenon. The success of modern science in the understanding and control of nature led early social scientists to the extrapolation of the methods of natural science to the realm of human behavior, again in the interests both of greater understanding and of control. The requisite value-freedom of the social sciences, coupled with an idealistic ethics, constituted a new reading of the relation of fact and value. But it is not the only one. Classic finalistic interpretations of nature involved the empirical discernment of regularities in nature as well. A reconceptualized social science, then, may involve renewed attention fo finality in nature itself. Considerations of nature and use are relevant here. The intelligibility of a social phenomenon is dependent upon the use people make of things and of themselves, particularly of human freedom, which is in Simon's view a kind of "superdeterminate rather than indeterminate" causality. It follows that an investigation into the philosophy of human nature will enhance our understanding of social facts.

Chapter 5 begins with a recapitulation of Simon's reservations concerning the "illusions" of social science. But is a "humanistic" counterattack against the social scientific project possible? The traditional tension between Christianity and humanism gives us pause. There is possibly little logical conflict between the two. But there is still the question of historical determination. The secularization of the eighteenth and nineteenth centuries can suggest that an integration of humanistic studies with Christian dogma is not a viable historical option.

Simon offers two suggestions. For one thing, a rejuvenated natural law theory may show the way, one in which natural law is properly illuminated by faith. The movements of the heart, so absolutely necessary to practical judgment, would find themselves mirrored in a moral science enlightened by revelation. Secondly, a new program of studies could more easily include modern classics as well as medieval Christian literature. The conflict then would be, not between Christianity and humanism, but between humanism and the technical culture spawned by eighteenth-century scientific optimism. The problem lies in subordinating technical culture as an instrumental means to the demands of a full humanism. Here, in the conclusion of this final practical syllogism, it is moral virtue that again will be decisive, in this case a supernatural virtue, the spirit of poverty. A program in humanistic studies then, faithful to the demands of Christianity on the one hand and to humanism on the other, and adequate to the need to subordinate modern technical culture, will include some attention to the masterpieces of Christian mysticism.

Yves Simon's last book has both perennial value and a high degree of contemporary relevance. It is clear that he perceived a huge theoretical "hole" in modern thought, one owing its origin to methodological and epistemological reductionism in early modern philosophy. The ideal of a unified science, by making the full range of human experience subject to a single methodology, forced into exile a practical knowledge that was neither science, on the one hand, nor technique, on the other. In turn, the social and political questions formerly considered part of an irreducible practical understanding, themselves became proper subject matter for the new unified science. The social sciences were born of this revolution in philosophical analysis. Simon's profound concern with concrete institutional forms of life and with large historical movements led him to the general position that many of the peculiar crises in recent and contemporary public life owe their causes to the loss of the classical theory of practical knowledge. Only a re-examination and reassessment of ancient accounts of this theme, especially as found in Aristotle and in Thomas Aquinas, could hope to reverse the reductionist tendencies of modern social science. This final book of Simon's is a challenging and indeed heroic effort to re-establish a unique place for practical knowledge in the analysis and resolution of human problems, both private and public. Certain contemporary tendencies enhance the timeliness and relevance of Simon's effort. At the present time there are, among philosophers and the general public, a renewed interest in virtue, a searching reappraisal of the limits of social scientific study, and an efflorescence of educational and cultural programs. Simon's focus on the intersection of wisdom and action can offer powerful and ramifying illumination in all these areas. His message is a simple one: the traditional concept of practical wisdom has been lost in the past four centuries of Western experience. Its recovery is an urgent need in our individual and social lives.

Assistance in the production of this volume has come from many sources. Early editorial efforts were begun by Ernest

Briones and Ralph Nelson. Vukan Kuic was helpful at several critical points, particularly in the final stages of preparation. The College of Humanities and Social Sciences of the University of South Carolina provided a summer research grant which allowed the major architecture of the piece to take form. Anthony O. Simon, director of the Yves R. Simon Institute, has been a source of generous encouragement. Above all, Mrs. Paule Y. Simon has offered continued and unflagging help. Without her understanding and persistence, much of this book would still be a series of notes and hopes. All deserve my recognition and warm thanks.

*Columbia, South Carolina*                    ROBERT J. MULVANEY

# 1

# The Ultimate Practical Judgment

OUR INQUIRY WILL BE CENTERED on an example, and the chosen example will be complex enough to exclude the illusions that simplicity might produce. Here is a true story: two geographers, who were also men of wisdom, had just heard of an accident in which several mountain climbers had died. Having no professional interest in the exploration of mountains, I somewhat shyly remarked that it was perhaps unlawful to expose one's life to such dangers for no other purposes than those served by the climbing of a peak. To my surprise the geographers blamed as plainly unethical the recklessness of mountain climbers.

Let us imagine a dialogue on this moral issue, and follow the track of practical thought all the way down to action itself. One character in the dialogue says that the immorality of extreme risk is particularly obvious when a man is in charge of a family. This occasions the remark that even a bachelor is not master and possessor of his own life. At this point someone declares that, after all, every human action or abstention involves risks; the important thing is that the seriousness of the risk should never be out of proportion to the worthiness of the cause. Then the conversation turns to the purposes of mountain climbing.

To accept danger in the service of science is better than lawful, especially if the benefit expected for theoretical and applied knowledge is great. Thus, mountain climbers, before they decide to go on an expedition, have a duty to weigh the probability of gathering valuable information. Here it is pointed out that many times, in the history of science, discoveries resulted from investigations that looked unpromising; thus it would be good and desirable to climb mountains even without any definite expectation. But someone holds that the balance of wisdom is being disrupted, and says, with a bit of indignation, that you cannot endanger your life unless there is a strong indication that significant results are at hand. Tired of such insistence on the service of science, another person shrugs his shoulders: mountain climbers care little for the improvement of knowledge but enjoy the thrill of danger and the intoxication of accomplishment. An austere moralist stresses that such is the case indeed, and, in an impassioned tone, censures the lightheartedness that drives people to early death for the sake of what is no more than vainglory.

However, is there not something to be said in favor of the attraction that dangerous life often exerts on generous natures? For the service of society, it is all important that many persons, especially among the young, should face the supreme sacrifice with cheerful readiness. Dangers that look absurd, like those incurred by jockeys and car racers, by mountain climbers and circus performers, are socially beneficial inasmuch as they keep alive, in young people especially, a readiness to die without which society would suffer every day from softness and cowardice, and be exposed to betrayal in times of crisis. But it is replied that great inconvenience attaches to any practice suggesting that human life is little valued. Bullfights have a bad reputation in this respect; they are said to foster disregard for man as well as cruelty toward animals.

The dialogue may go on for a long time without ceasing to be reasonable. Idle talk is not yet in sight. All that has been said so far is true, and much more truth can be relevantly voiced on the ethical problem raised by the dangers of mountain climbing. The statements made conflict with one another, yet this does not mean that any of them is false. They express contrasting aspects of the issue: precisely, a wise deliberation gives keen attention to contrasts, and the most important task of wisdom often is to preserve a multiplicity of goods in spite of their opposition.

So far, all the rules brought in are general in character and lie at a great distance from action. But consider the problem of a sportsman who has just been invited to join a team determined to ascend a challenging peak. For his deliberation to be faultless, all the propositions of the preceding dialogue must play a role—though, perhaps, in merely virtual and implicit fashion. And many more particular questions are of essential relevance: granted that it is lawful to take some risk for the service of science and the glory of sportsmanship, what about the particularities of this individual case? Is the moment properly chosen? Whether we are or are not in the season of avalanches makes all the difference between foolishness and reasonableness. What about the guide? Is he experienced, serious-minded, temperate? How was his reputation established? By reliable witness or by hearsay? A conclusion is reached when and only when full assent is given to a judgment which, whether by affirmation or negation, immediately touches action. Let us suppose that this judgment is affirmative. The sportsman is equipped, walks toward his companions, and says, "Everything looks fine, fellows, I'll go with you." And off they go.

We were already definitely within the system of practical thought when we were pondering, at a rather high level of abstraction, such general duties as those concerning the preservation of one's life and the necessary readiness to accept death for a worthy cause. But the practical character of thought has obviously increased with the transition to more concrete subjects and to questions closer to the final decision. The ultimate degree of practicality is attained by the judgment which, except in the case of interference by some external force, cannot not be followed by action. Such is the *command* that a sportsman gives himself when he walks toward his companions and declares that he is ready to go. It is by the study of the ultimate and ultimately practical judgment that we propose to establish the fundamentals of the theory of practical wisdom.

## Practical Judgment as the Form of Action

This judgment, metaphorically described as touching action immediately, is, in a direct, proper, and unqualified sense, the *form of action*. Therefore it is as practical as action itself.[1]

The notion of form, though primarily relative to the explanation of physical change, retains here all its signification. Within a complex reality, the form is the component by reason of which the complex is what it is rather than anything else, by reason of which it belongs to a genus and a species rather than to any other genus and species. The act of determinately willing to do this—e.g., of willing to go on a mountain climbing expedition, not hypothetically, but factually and here and now—is what it is, is constituted in its identity, is distinguished from whatever it is not, by the ultimate practical judgment. A practical judgment is ultimate inasmuch as, all hypothetical considerations being transcended, it has the character of a command. Action and the judgment that commands it are no more external to each other than the marble statue and the shape by reason of which it is a statue of Hercules rather than one of Apollo. Action—I speak not of any action elicited by a human being, but of those distinctly human acts which proceed from rational apprehension, deliberation, and choice—includes the ultimate judgment by which it is determined, just as a physical thing includes the form that, by being present within it, causes it to be what it is.

There is such a significant contrast between thought and action that the notion of practical thought may seem to bear the character of a compromise; it looks like a lump made of principles that qualify each other and hold each other in check. Indeed, at a distance from the concrete, as in the case of a universal rule considered as universal, thought falls short of total practicality.[2] But when the distance between thought and action is nil, when thought has come down into the complex of human action to constitute its form, it is described as practical in an absolutely appropriate sense. To sum up, let it be said that the expression "the practical order" designates both action itself and practical thought. All practical judgments belong to the order of practical thought, but the ultimate one, and it alone among judgments, belongs also, intrinsically and necessarily, to the order of action. The ultimate practical judgment is the form of action and the final expression of thought in its practical function. Through it principles come to exist in the world of action. The principle that deposits ought to be returned exists in my action through the command that I give myself as I write a check in the name of my creditor. Through the efficacy of the last practical judgment, practical principles come to possess in act the character of forms of action which, by their very constitution as practical principles, they tend to assume.

## The Synthesis of Practical Judgment

The ultimate practical judgment involves a unique synthesis, namely, the putting together of a certain "that" and the act of existing. Indeed, a theoretical judgment may express, in a diversity of ways, the synthesis of essence and "to be"; it may express it as fictitious, as possible, as actual, and as present in actual experience. What is unique in the synthesis that the last practical judgment involves is its decisive *weight*, the actuality of the tendency that it conveys, the drive by which it carries a "that" toward the action of existing, in short, the unconditional fashion in which it unites the formal cause and the final cause, the object of cognition and the object of appetition.[3] Let this synthesis be called the *synthesis of realization*, and let us remark that it determines, all the way down from the highest principles of the practical order, a synthetic behavior in sharp contrast with the ways of theoretical thought.

In order to understand what is meant by the traditional proposition that theoretical knowledge proceeds analytically and practical knowledge synthetically, we must go back to what is fundamental in the notion of analysis and in the characteristic features of theoretical thought. "Analysis" is often understood as a synonym of "decomposition" and often connotes the picture of things disjoined and scattered which offer to the mind only the dead parts of what used to be a splendid and living reality. It is analysis so understood that is scoffed at in the famous lines of Mephistopheles to the student:

> Whoever wants to know and to describe
> a living thing,
>
> First endeavors to drive the spirit
> out of it,
>
> Then he has the parts in his hand,

> But unfortunately the spiritual link
> is missing.[4]

These lines are an adequate motto for the many schools and trends of thought which, in the last three generations, have been reacting against the tendency toward universal resolution into elements: holism, vitalism, the Gestalt theory, intuitionism of various descriptions, pragmatism, *Charakterkunde*, the stream of consciousness of William James, the deep self of Bergson, the action of Blondel, the existentialism of Sartre, etc.[5] Such indefatigable, never-ending reactions bear witness to the lasting foundation of that which is reacted against. Holistic philosophies are up against a power that will never acknowledge defeat, for, in spite of all shortcomings, it certainly holds its own in vast areas of research. It is of the greatest significance to determine whether the tendency toward universal decomposition into parts, which threatens to kill the unity of things, is an essential feature of theoretical science. That it characterizes demonstrative knowledge, science in the traditional and customary sense of the term, is a major tenet of Bergsonism; according to this philosophy, whose profound intention is not pragmatic but contemplative,[6] real and living totalities are not apprehended, the spiritual link of things is irretrievably broken, and utilitarian bias remains in control of our approaches, as long as conceptual delineations, decompositions, distinctions, and abstractions are not transcended in intuitive insights akin and adequate to the primordial *élan* by which things come into being and are kept in motion.

Yet inasmuch as it characterizes theoretical science, analysis is primarily concerned, not with the relation of whole to part, but with the relation of effect to cause and of consequence to principle. To analyze, or to resolve, is to render a situation intelligible by tracing an effect to its cause or a consequence to its principle. But there are two reasons why analysis is often associated with a process of decomposition into parts. The first is that experience generally presents us with contingent aggregates that must be divided into their components in order to find the processes of essential causality which alone are explanatory. It commonly happens that these processes are not initially free from contingent associations and have to be isolated by our industry, both rational and experimental. Divisions, subdivisions, distinctions often subtle are so many operations preparatory to the analysis that is characteristic of theoretical thought.

When explanation follows the line of material causality, a new relation may appear between analysis and decomposition, for the parts are the material cause of the whole. The analysis of a thing into its material causes may coincide with its decomposition into its parts. The notion of analysis will be more steadily associated with that of decomposition when material causes supply the prevalent method of explanation. Such was the case of Western culture at the time when biological, psychological, moral, and social sciences took it for granted that the best they could do was to follow, as exactly as possible, the pattern set by the physical and chemical sciences. Here the materialistic method assumes the form of mechanism, and arrangements, movements, and rearrangements of particles are expected to account for all structures and processes. The criticism that gave birth to the holistic trends predominant in contemporary psychology was particularly aimed at theories designed to explain mental life by primary components patterned after the elements, atoms, and molecules of the chemists.

When the cause to which an effect is traced has the character of a whole, when a situation is rendered intelligible by the properties of the whole rather than by the nature and arrangement of the parts, the method is just as certainly analytical as in the case of analysis into parts. In both cases what calls for explanation is treated by being resolved, or analyzed, into that which has the power of explanation. Contemporary epistemology is crowded with remarks concerning the many operations of synthetic and constructive nature that are constantly performed by theoretical science. These remarks, or most of them, certainly hold, but they do not invalidate the proposition that theoretical science is characterized by an analytical procedure, for, whether it sets things apart or puts them together, theoretical thought remains primarily concerned with explanatory knowledge, i.e., with the analysis of effects and consequences into causes and principles.

Even when it stays at a great distance from action, practical thought is governed by a law of completeness that is derived from the metaphysical nature of the good. The act to be posited in existence, whatever it may be, is driven into existence by a desire. It is an end or a means to an end; in either case it has the character of a good and cannot be what it is supposed to be save by the proper operation of all its causes. By the law of Dionysius,[7] "The good is brought about by a cause possessed of integrality, whereas a multitude of defects, though relative to parts, issues in evil." In the example just described, it is clear that the act of joining a team of mountain climbers is not good, that the judgment that commands such an act is not what it is supposed to be, unless a multiplicity of conditions is put together so as to give the cause at work this character of completeness and integrality. The wise decision, in this example, puts together, synthesizes, the worthy purpose and the not excessive danger, moderation concerning such aims as the glory of achievement and the thrill of danger (which can so easily impair the soundness of judgment), the appropriate season and the adequate state of health, the skill of the guide and his moral dependability, the family responsibilities that weigh against readiness to face danger, etc. Anything lacking in this combination of conditions suffices to render the judgment imprudent. A slightly upset stomach by causing dizziness, or a sprained ankle, may entail disaster for an entire team of mountain climbers. No wonder that men dedicated to theoretical studies are reputed to be at a disadvantage when they have to be practical: their habits of thought are such that they have a tendency to leave out a few of the data or factors whose combination is indispensable for successful action. They are used to an order of things where what matters is the working of essential causes and their relations to their essential effects. It takes a great deal of versatility to be excellent both at the methods of abstraction, distinction, isolation, and consideration in solitude which serve explanation, and at the methods of synthesis, composition, and complex consideration, oblivious of nothing, aware of the significance of the most minute accidents, which are the ways of wisdom in the life of action. The synthesis of command and realization is characterized by decisiveness and completeness: decisiveness concerns the relations of the *that* to the act of existing; completeness, the constitution of the *that*. In phases antecedent to command, the practical synthesis is both indecisive and incomplete.

## Nature and Use

The notion of use is of such significance in the theory of practical knowledge that no effort should be spared to make it entirely clear. Let us, first, consider examples evidencing the relation between good and evil in physical reality and in human use. External things, whether they be things of nature or works of human industry, admit of being good or poor in a physical sense and admit of being put to a good or to a bad use. It is possible to make a good use of a good car and a bad use of a good car and a bad use of a poor car and a good use of a poor car. Turning to the powers of man himself: it is obviously possible to make a good use of good eyesight, and a poor use of it, and a poor use of poor eyesight and a good use of it. What holds for a sensorial faculty holds equally for memory, imagination, intelligence, and the will itself. It is possible to make a good use of a strong will and a poor use of a strong will and a good use of a weak will.
. . . We might be tempted to say that there is no connection between good in nature and good in use, or between evil in nature and evil in use. Yet some thought-provoking cases warn us that evil in nature may constitute, in various ways, an inclination toward evil in use. Correspondingly, the danger of evil use may be removed, or at least decreased, by some perfections of nature. The proposition that it is possible to make a good use of a poor car can be challenged when what is poor about the car is the condition of its brakes. With a car whose brakes do not work safely, the only good use is, under almost all circumstances, abstaining from use, and we consider that it is improper to keep in one's garage a car whose brakes are not safe; the availability of such a thing is a temptation to indulge in improper use. Thus, even though the thing under consideration be external to man, a certain defect of nature may cause a tendency toward wrong use. This assumes extreme seriousness when the thing suffering from a defect of nature is the human appetite itself,

whose act is an inclination. Consider emotional aberrations. They may be totally traceable to accidents of nature and in no degree to bad use. But because they are of such nature as to admit of no good use, and because their dynamic character constitutes an urge, and perhaps a violent one, toward use and bad use, the law of good use is greatly concerned with their being silenced or uprooted.

So far, we have been considering use in its *human* sense; we have spoken of good and bad use in relation to man, that is, in relation to the ends that are those of man considered precisely as man. Let it be noticed that use may be relative not to man as man but to the particular quality of some power or expertness, and that good and evil in use may be relative not to the ends of man but to this particular quality. A grammarian is excellently qualified to make grammatical mistakes if he pleases to, and a highly skilled chemical engineer is the logical man for sabotaging a chemical factory. Whereas virtue involves an essential tendency toward good human use, the neutrality of expertness is twofold: of any art or technique (*a*) it is possible to make a humanly good use, or a bad use, or no use at all, and (*b*) it is also possible to make a use that is right or wrong from the very point of view of art or technique.[8]

It is entirely clear that the judgment concerning use is closer to action than any judgment about nature, and that, within the limits of voluntariness, the judgment concerning *human* use is closer to action than the judgment concerning *particular* use. The ultimate practical judgment involves the consideration of human use, and the disposition that makes for excellence in ultimate practical judgment is not a mere skill, expertness, art, or technique, but a virtue in the full sense of the term. The mastery of an art makes it possible to perform excellently the operations of this art, if and only if this is what the craftsman pleases to do. But, once more, an art can be used against man and even against its own purposes. On the contrary, a virtue properly so called is, in the words of St. Augustine, "a quality . . . of which no one makes a wrong use."[9] It is impossible to make a wrong use of a virtue because a virtue procures the right use as well as the right quality of whatever is subject to its control. And not to make use of virtue when circumstances demand that use be made of it is contrary to the essential inclination of virtue. Of all the intellectual habitus, prudence alone is a virtue properly so called—which indeed implies that it is not purely intellectual.

## The Truth of Practical Judgment

The problem of truth in the practical judgment is best approached by asking in what sense a judgment immediately relative to action, a command, can attain certainty. Suppose that the heir to a considerable estate hears disquieting reports on the methods used by his grandfather in the making of his fortune. If the reports are true, he is not the legitimate owner of this estate which he has treated as his, in good faith, for some time. Although the doubt is slight, the honest fellow feels obligated to inquire. After patient and conscientious research, the doubt has not become more serious, but it has not been completely removed. It proved impossible to find the only document that could establish finally whether he or someone else is the legitimate owner of the estate. A time comes when it would be wrong to spend more time and energy on an inquiry that seems bound never to give any decisive result. All will agree that after such conscientious endeavors the factual possessor ought to conclude "I am entitled to keep this estate." Justice is fully satisfied provided he is determined to accept the consequences, no matter how unpleasant, of a possible discovery of the lost document. How shall we interpret the proposition "I am entitled to keep this estate" in terms of truth and certitude? By hypothesis this proposition is not in certain agreement with the facts, for these have not been established certainly. The lost document may turn up, and reveal that the doubt was well-grounded, that the estate actually belongs to someone else. Then the honest man will confess that he is not entitled to keep this estate. The proposition that terminated his inconclusive inquiry, "I am entitled to keep this estate," proves to be at variance with facts. In a way it was false, but not in every way, for no one would declare that a man erred when, after a conscientious inquiry, he concluded, in accordance with all available evidence, that he was entitled to retain an estate. In view of the evidence available, his decision was what it was supposed to be. It was good. It fully agreed with the requirements of justice. It was the decision that any honest man had to make in such a case. It was the proper rule of action under the circumstances; for action cannot be ruled according to unavailable evidence.

And thus we are led to understand that a practical judgment admits of being true or false in more than one sense. It may be true by conformity to the factual state of affairs: this is the primary, the theoretical, the unqualified meaning of truth. In that sense a practical judgment always falls short of certainty inasmuch as any practical situation involves contingencies that defeat the most earnest endeavor to establish the conformity of our judgments to the factual state of things contingent, i.e., of things that can be otherwise than they are. In ordinary life we forget about this uncertainty of our prudence because we are busy, because we are sensible, and because we are willing to take chances. Yet the possibility of disastrous discrepancies between our decisions and the real state of affairs is threatening at all times, with death as a common effect of undetectable error. It would be unreasonable to eat food prepared by people notoriously eager to cause my death, but most of the time the sensible and virtuous thing, when mealtime has come, is to take food without thought of poison. True, once in a while you hear of whole families having died as a result of an accident in the preparation of food. The probability is extremely small, say, one in many million, but between such a small probability and the elimination of all adverse chance, the distance is no smaller than between the yes and the no. Adjustment of life, good sense, good judgment consists, to a large extent, in an ability to know where to stop in the indispensable quest for a certainty that indeed cannot be attained in the world of contingency in which our actions take place. Whether or not our food contains poison is worth ascertaining. But if we really mean to establish with certainty the conformity of the proposition "This food contains no poison" to reality, death by starvation is our certain destiny. The same considerations hold for all aspects of human life. We have to fight our way between careless action without appropriate inquiry and a neurotic search for certainty in uncertain matters.

Yet our eagerness for certainty finds satisfaction in the world of action inasmuch as the practical judgment, over and above an inevitably weak quality of theoretical truth, is capable of another type of truth, of a practical truth, of a truth that becomes it properly as a practical judgment, of a truth that is one not of cognition but of direction, of a truth that consists, not in conformity to a real state of affairs, but in conformity to the demands of an honest will, in conformity to the inclination of a right desire.[10] The man who doubted his ownership, having done his best to clear up the case, was judging in accordance with the requirements of honesty when he decided that he was entitled to retain the estate—with a firm determination, however, to return it in the event new evidence should invalidate his reasonable conclusion. For a judgment that is unqualifiedly practical, the proper way to be true is to be true in a practical sense; that is, to be true as a rule of action. The genuineness of a rule of action is its conformity to intention, provided, of course, that intention itself is genuine, that is, relative to the proper end. Posit the intention of the proper end and posit, in relation to the means, a judgment in unqualified agreement with the genuine intention. This judgment is the true rule of action; it is true as a rule of action, it possesses truth of direction, with absolute certainty—no matter how badly it may remain affected by doubt when considered in relation to the real state of affairs—in other words, when considered in its theoretical truth.[11]

Again, the rightness of desire is in no case compatible with indifference to the real condition of the factors involved in the bringing about of the intended good. The practical judgment that asserts that such and such a course of action will lead to the end cannot be established with complete certainty so far as its relation to facts is concerned. But the probable agreement of the practical conclusion with what does exist and with what is going to happen in reality is something that right desire necessarily demands. Sometimes this probable agreement is sought through slow and leisurely research, which may spread over years, and sometimes it is sought in an extremely short space of time. At the wheel of a car a decision upon which the lives of several persons depend may have to be made in a split second.

When the desire is right, when the genuine end is properly intended, which implies that there is conscientious inquiry into the real state of affairs, practical judgment can be reasonably expected to be followed by successful action. A decision made in full agreement with right desire may turn out to be disastrous. But constant agreement with right desire—in other words, constant certainty in practical truth—normally implies a high ratio of agreement with facts and consequently entails a high ratio of success in the discharge of our duties. A statesman may well meet failure as a result of a decision in full agreement with right desire, but if his decisions steadily agree with the virtues that make up statesmanship, they will, in many cases, actually preserve and promote the good of the community. Notice, however, that the normal expectation of success, whether in politics or in any other domain of practical wisdom, can be upset by more than one kind of accident. Thus, in the management of a family, the wisdom of a decision can be invalidated by an unpredictable outbreak of disease; there is no guarantee that a succession of equally conscientious decisions will not be invalidated by a succession of equally unpredictable outbreaks. Once in a while we notice that the prudence of the wisest is defeated by a bewildering series of such misfortunes as diseases, transportation accidents, betrayals, etc. In these cases the cause of failure is external to the agent; such dark series can be likened to long successions of identical occurrences in games of chance: they are improbable and happen rarely. More significant are the factors of failure which lie in the agent himself without impairing the rightness of his desire and the agreement of his decisions with his right desire. Let us consider typical examples of these factors.

First comes involuntary ignorance. Without any fault of his, without anything that would impair the rightness of his desire, a man may not know what should be known in order for his decisions to be possessed of highly probable agreement with reality. This often happens in individual conduct, and it more often happens in the government of communities. There may and there may not be awareness of ignorance. If the person is not aware that he is short of indispensable information, he has no means to correct his limitations, and if he is aware of his harmful ignorance, he still may be unable to do much about it, at least for some time. By reason of his good will, he is eager to procure the help of better-informed advisers, but it often happens that no advice can substitute for personal acquaintance with the data of a problem and with the possible answers. In the case of a leader, honest awareness of harmful ignorance sometimes demands that he resign his duties. But a leader is not always free to resign. Thus, in leadership as well as in the government of oneself, frequent failure may follow judgments that fully agree with right desire and are possessed of certainty in practical truth.

The uncertainty of our prudences appears frightful as we consider the great variety of factors that can adversely affect the relation of practical judgment to reality. Involuntary ignorance in a leader does not result only from failure to get information that, next time, can be procured by consulting the proper memorandum or the proper man. On a deeper level, it may result from such deficiencies as lack of memory for names, faces, or traits of individual character; slow associations and slow processes of thought; inadequacy in the complex of abilities that we confusedly but meaningfully call instinct, knack, intuitive craft, practical sense; cold temperament, entailing privation of the warnings and suggestions that emotional intuition alone can procure; exposure to disturbance by irrational inclinations and aversions.

Concerning this last factor, one might be tempted to say that right desire should procure immunity to such disturbances, but in order for this remark to hold, the rightness that is spoken of should pertain not only to desire but also to all the conditions and instruments involved in its operation. In fact, one may be a man of good will and right desire and yet suffer from significant imperfection with respect to these conditions and instruments. Likewise, a violin player may be a great artist and yet give a poor performance because of defects in the material conditions and in the instrument of his art. This famous virtuoso may not do so well as expected just because he has been tired by a long trip, or because the only available violin is a relatively poor thing, or because the physical circumstances of the auditorium adversely affect the working of his instrument. A man of right desire will strive to protect his judgment against all emotional disturbances, but to expect that he will be entirely successful is as illusory as to hope that both the virtuoso and his instrument will always be in perfect shape. In fact, it is much easier to keep a virtuoso in shape and a violin in tune than to keep a man of excellent will free from deceitful emotions, and free from the blind spots that may result from a lack of emotions.

Let attention be called, in particular, to emotional disturbances that are social in origin. These are the more difficult to avoid since they proceed from energies whose uninhibited operation matters primordially for the soundness of practical judgment, most of all when the welfare of communities is involved. We would not trust a leader who would appear to us as a fine individual disconnected from the social factors of inclination and aversion, judgment and action. Always supposing that his will is good, we would feel less confident if we realized that neither family traditions, nor historical trends, nor collective representations and drives are of much weight in his deliberations and decisions. We consider that the springs of a personality are inevitably weak unless they derive power from what is most vital in a community, or in several communities. Accordingly, we want a statesman to be a man of traditions, a man rooted in the history of a variety of groups, a man inspired by the needs, the ambitions, the regrets, the defeats, the great memories, and even the myths of the groups to which he belongs. We know that without all this social and historical substance his personality would be shallow and his leadership petty. But a discipline that would submit to a perfectly rational order all the forces of society and history existent in an ample soul without crushing any of them would be an almost superhuman marvel of balance and harmony. And unless such an improbable marvel is realized, the agreement of the practical judgment with the actual state of things is not immune to disturbance secretly originating in perhaps remote parts of the space and duration of social existence.

## Ultimate Practical Judgment

### Judgment by Inclination

The practical judgment, whose proper perfection is truth by agreement with right desire, is ultimately determined not by cognition but by inclination, and its determination is certain if the inclination that ultimately determines it is right. Any decision of great consequence, if it is made in the midst of particularly obscure circumstances, is accompanied by the realization that all the reasons adduced are insufficient. It has been prepared by arguments of our own and by arguments proposed by advisers, by arguments that agreed with our spontaneous dispositions and by arguments that were eagerly considered, out of a sense of duty, in spite of their being sharply at variance with our spontaneity. Arguments filled much space in our consciousness; they were active and restless, perhaps noisy and furious, yet they did not entail any conclusion by logical necessity. After they had displayed their impressive power, it was still possible for objections to silence them and to develop a fury of their own. But a time came when we realized that the thing to do was to dismiss passions and prejudices, to rank as nothing our pride, our covetousness, our laziness and our anger, to transcend our subjectivity, to overcome the weight of our own selves and, in a great act of good will, to seek identification with the movement of justice toward what is right, to lose ourselves in an unrestricted desire that the movement of our resolution be one with the movement of justice. The antecedent consideration of arguments did not, then, seem to have been irrelevant or unnecessary: clearly, it was demanded by, and presupposed to, the generous act of good will which procures the final determination. It was necessary and good that arguments be thoroughly considered, but they had to be transcended if certain conclusions were to emerge. The strongest arguments were inconclusive, and it was not by an argument that the conclusion was brought about. Answer to the ultimate question was obtained by listening to an inclination. The intellect, here, is the disciple of love. The object of the practical judgment is one that cannot be grasped by looking at it. It is delivered by love to the docile intellect. As John of St. Thomas says in words of Augustinian beauty, *Amor transit in conditionem objecti,* "Love takes over the role of object."[12]

The practical judgment is, within our familiar experience, the most certain as well as the clearest case of affective knowledge. Let it be remarked that affective dispositions may play a very important part in the genesis of knowledge without concerning knowledge in any intrinsic way. Extrinsic does not mean unimportant. To be sure, in all departments of knowledge, industry, honesty, docility, ambition, perseverance, resiliency, interest in and love for the subject are major conditions of success; these conditions remain entirely extrinsic. They are needed in algebra as well as in geography, and yet none would hold that the conclusions of the algebraist are determined by his virtuous inclinations. Some fields of knowledge are reputed to require, besides general qualities of application, a certain loftiness of character, a particular freedom from passions, a generous readiness to accept the sacrifices that the acknowledgment of truth may require. Let us assume, in accordance with common belief, that such is generally the condition of philosophy: it does not follow that philosophic knowledge is in any sense or degree an affective knowledge. The part played by affective dispositions in philosophy remains entirely extrinsic. These dispositions do not concern the philosophic assent. To take a simple example, moral debasement may cause an atheistic attitude, and an atheistic attitude may occasion a panpsychistic interpretation of nature. But the moral soundness which procures freedom from such interferences does not in any way determine assent to the propositions that make up the philosophy of natural finality.[13]

In the case of the practical judgment, there is affective knowledge in the intrinsic and most appropriate sense of this expression. Between the yes and the no, it is the right inclination which dictates the answer, "yes" in the case of positive inclination, "no" in the case of aversion. Haste, rationalistic illusions and ambitions, and unfamiliarity with mysteries that are indeed hidden in their very familiarity make it somewhat difficult to achieve complete awareness of the overwhelming fact that in all phases of our moral life we run into issues that inclinations alone can decide. We cannot question that in some cases the light comes from an affective movement, but we are tempted to believe that these are more or less exceptional. It would be helpful to analyze some of the cases in which the deciding power of the heart is plain and then to examine, in the light of the plainer case, the situations that are not so plain.

The following story will bring to mind familiar experiences of affective knowledge: An honest businessman is visited by a fellow who obviously masters the rules of his game. His proposals seem to be financially safe as well as profitable and, in spite of the suspicions generally attaching to financial plans that look so good, perfectly honest. So, when the honest and experienced businessman is asked why he rejected the proposal without further inquiry, the ways of rational argumentation will not silence his critics. Yet his "no" is resolute and definitive. It seems that he did not even hesitate to dismiss the proposal and the would-be partner. Instead of explanations, he uses metaphors expressing aversion. "Yes, it is not easy to see what is wrong with his plan but sometimes you can smell things that you cannot see."[14] But it is not every day that one has to do with gentlemen whose craft routs arguments and can be defeated only by a sensitiveness that words cannot express. It seems that in daily life argument takes care of our problems. Let us see what becomes of this impression when facts are examined closely. Today I got up at seven. This is trivial indeed, yet I remember that when it was time to set my alarm clock I hesitated between longer hours of work and badly needed rest. I thought of getting up very early in order to have plenty of work done before noon. Fatigue made me change my mind. But how did I know that I should not arise early in spite of my fatigue? How did I know that I should not make a greater concession to my need for rest and get up still later? To be sure, it is not in the power of any argument to establish a necessary connection between the judgment that I should get up at seven and any necessary principle. The trivial decision to get up at seven is made by inclination as certainly, though not so noticeably, as that of doing no business with a man who causes repugnance in the heart of the just.

Let us now consider the condition that must be satisfied for the determination of the judgment to be safely entrusted to affective inclinations. The expression "wishful thinking" conveys the suggestion that whenever thought is influenced by wish it ceases to be reliable. Thinking according to one's wishes is reputed to be a casual way of conducting our thoughts, and one that is probably at variance with reality. Is it possible for our wishes, and our aversions as well, to achieve such steady agreement with the objects of right intention that an objective demand for assent be expressed by a positive inclination, and an objective demand for a negation by an aversion and a feeling of repugnance? Is it possible for our heart, i.e., our will and our sense appetite, to be in such steady agreement with the object of virtue that our inclinations and aversions no longer be exposed to the arbitrariness of subjectivity but assume the reliable power of an object?

We answer this question whenever we declare, or imply, that a judgment determined by a virtuous inclination is necessarily in agreement with virtue. If a person is known for unflinching dedication to justice, we think that his example can be safely followed, in difficult problems of justice, provided all the relevant circumstances are the same in his case and ours. We trust that the instincts of people whom we know to be really virtuous cannot be at variance with what virtue demands. Clearly, there exists a harmony, a sympathy, a dynamic unity, a community of nature, in short, a *connaturality*, between the virtuous heart and the requirements of virtue. When justice demands that a proposal be answered by "no," how could the heart of the just fail to elicit an act of aversion? The nature of the just heart, *qua* just, is the essence of justice. The practical judgment, in order to be true and certain, ought to proceed not by logical connection with axioms (such a connection is impossible in contingent matters), but by way of virtuous inclination. This judgment is an act of knowledge through affective connaturality.

At the end of our remarks on use, it was pointed out that the disposition in charge of the ultimate practical judgment cannot be a mere habitus: it is a virtue, i.e., a habitus that procures excellence in exercise as well as in quality. Again, the last practical judgment is the form of human action and involves, over and above all excellence of nature and of particular use, the requirement of excellence in *human* use. Prudence, the intellectual habitus that alone can guarantee the truth of the last practical judgment and the soundness of action, is a virtue in the most proper sense of this term.

Let us elaborate on the character of prudence as a virtue. (*a*) A quality of the practical understanding, prudence presupposes a system of virtuous inclinations inasmuch as these alone can steadily cause a judgment possessed of practical truth. Briefly, moral virtues are needed to procure the good *quality* of the practical judgment. (*b*) Since the practical judgment determines the actual use of man's free choice, the habitus which makes for its steady excellence must cause the right exercise of the judgment as well as its truth. Whereas the habitus of art is not impaired by one's failure to make use of it at the proper time, it is clear that it would be imprudent, i.e., contrary to prudence, to refrain from judging when the circumstances demand that there be judgment. And whereas it is possible to make a wrong use of art, the notion of an immoral use of prudence is as obviously self-contradictory as that of an immoral use of justice or temperance. (*c*) The system of good inclinations required for the virtuous steadiness of the prudent judgment is a *complete* one. This implies, first, that nothing short of virtue properly so called can procure the needed rightness of the desire; good dispositions which have not yet attained the status of virtue do not suffice. It implies, second, that all moral virtues are needed to guarantee prudent judgment in any domain of morality. It would be pleasant to imagine that in order to judge prudently in matters of justice it suffices to be just. But assuming—fictitiously—that it is possible to possess justice without possessing the other moral virtues, let us see what would be the condition of judgment about problems of justice in a soul deprived of courage and temperance. So long as the benefit to be derived from unjust choice is not very great, the weight of covetousness and cowardice is not too badly felt and lucid judgment is not impossible. A man temperamentally inclined toward the just, but afflicted with disorderly passions, can be expected to distinguish the just from the unjust when the matter does not arouse his greed and his fear, in other words, when the matter is of insignificant weight. But when the right choice entails heavy sacrifice, lust and fear cause the confusion of judgment and color the unjust with an appearance of justice. This is how moral virtues are interconnected in prudence. Their interdependence has its center in the *judgment* which constitutes the form of their acts, for this is a judgment by inclination whose soundness, in any domain of morality, is impaired by any significant defect in the system of our inclinations. Another reason why moral virtues are interconnected is that each of them needs modes procured by the others. To resist the temptation of injustice often takes much courage and a steady practice of moderation. It is not possible to be just without being courageous and temperate. A cowardly person can be trusted in matters of justice so long as the pressure is not too strong, but we know that under high pressure he will, say, break his word. Such restricted, precarious, and hypothetical justice is not a virtue. Justice, in the state of virtue, possesses a character of strength procured by fortitude as well as a character of moderation procured by temperance.[15]

The theory of the interconnection of virtues entails the conclusion that the cost of prudence is frightfully high. No wonder that much ingenuity is spent finding ways out of such a predicament, albeit with the complicity of the most improbable illusions. Socratic theories indentifying science and virtue, casuistic extensions of moral science into the domain of contingency, the calculus of probabilities replacing good judgment in magistrates and rulers,[16] a social science that would say what we need to know in order to make our societies rational—these products of rationalistic optimism, no matter how fantastic, are easier to accept than the prospect of having to acquire all virtues.

Notice, however, that prudence can be genuine without all moral virtues being possessed in an equal degree of excellence. There is no justice without fortitude, but a man may be excellently just without having more fortitude than is needed to avoid grave acts of cowardice; his justice can be distinguished in spite of his fortitude's being merely sufficient.

Contrary to the stiff attitude which found expression in Stoicism and in several modern systems of morality—Calvinism, Jansenism, Kantism . . . —a good quality that does not possess the firmness of virtue, a good moral quality by way of mere disposition, can be a thing of great value. It is mostly against the background of an optimistic vision of nature and mankind that the attitude conveyed by the words "all or nothing" succeeds in making itself acceptable. If we realized that nature is a tragedy rather than an opera and that no being in nature is so badly exposed to failure as man, we would be more willing to understand that incomplete failure, partial success, precarious accomplishment, uncertain achievement are very much better than the state of utter failure which would have been hardly evitable, in the overwhelming majority of cases, without the helpful circumstances procured by religion and by civilization. A coward cannot be an honest man in the full sense of the term, for an honest man does not break his word, even under high pressure, whereas a coward breaks his when the pressure is too strong. However, if he yields only to very strong pressure, if his insufficient fortitude suffices under ordinary circumstances and proves inadequate only when the pressure is exceptional, many transactions go on according to the rule of honesty. Under the better circumstances, such imperfect honesty, not a virtue indeed, acts as a preparation to virtue. Altogether, the good moral quality which does not have the firmness of virtue is valuable in three respects. (1) Considered in itself, such a disposition procures a frequency of good actions under average circumstances, and this is much better than complete casualness. (2) A frequency of good action is of immense importance for society. Inasmuch as it contributes to the stable good of the community, the unstable good of these dispositions is, so to speak, lifted above its own capacity. (3) With regard to the individual agent, the imperfection of these dispositions is normally a way to virtue. It is only by accident that complete moral debasement favors conversion to ethical excellence more than dispositions to virtue would.

## The Incommunicability of the Ultimate Practical Judgment

Inasmuch as the ultimate practical judgment admits of no logical connection with any rational premises, it is, strictly speaking, incommunicable. For the proper understanding of this proposition, we must bear in mind the difference between the cognitions whose communicability is restricted, no matter how narrowly, in a purely factual way, and those that are incommunicable by nature. Demonstration entails communicability. This is so clear that whenever we observe persistent failure in communication, we are tempted to think that demonstration has not been achieved, and is perhaps impossible. The inference certainly holds with regard to the connection between demonstration and essential communicability. But if communicability and its opposite are taken in a *factual* sense, we can readily understand that demonstration does not always imply a promise of communication. To say the least, it does not promise that the assent of many will be obtained. Actual failure to win consensus does not necessarily evidence failure to demonstrate. Scientists, as opposed to philosophers, are famous for their ability to agree. True, the sciences become every day less communicable to the layman, but he is completely reassured by the agreement that conspicuously holds among the experts. According to Descartes, the disagreements of the philosophers merely meant that the right method had not yet been recognized; fortunately, the time had come when it could be promulgated in four simple rules. Today, it is almost universally held that the lack of consensus among philosophers evidences philosophy's inability to attain the condition of demonstrative knowledge. But the uncertainty of this opinion is brought out by the simple remark that *if* philosophic propositions were all demonstrated in the most rigorous way, many factors that are common and lasting, though completely accidental, would still account for the philosophers' failure to agree.

The incommunicability of the last practical judgment results from the affective and non-logical character of the act that determines this judgment. I may be completely unable to convince my neighbor that my decision is sound, even though it be certainly such. As a matter of fact, it is only at rare moments that the man of practical wisdom has to fight his way in solitude, amidst puzzled companions who say that they cannot understand him. Why this does not happen more frequently is a significant question.[17] Let us try to see what causes men often to agree quite readily in matters of action even though the last practical judgment never can be logically connected with principles that would necessitate the assent of all.

(*a*) For one thing, it often happens that the individual conditions of our acts comprise no particular feature of relevance. This can be easily shown by comparing normal with extraordinary circumstances. When a catastrophe has upset social relations, people may argue as to whether uncommon ways in the use of food and shelter have become legitimate, or still are what they would be if all were normal, viz., sheer injustice. Under normal circumstances the principle that stealing is wrong leads all of us, without further ado, to the conclusion that we should not take groceries without paying for them or break into our neighbor's home. In such matters, we call normal, or ordinary, the circumstances that comprise no particular feature of relevance. All the relevant features are general. We are unaware of the part played by the affective determination of our judgment because the absence of any particular difficulty makes it possible for us to recognize at once the right essences and the wrong ones in the concrete situations. But a big fire, an earthquake, a tornado, a flood, a riot, or a war may cause new difficulties and particular features of relevance to arise, and then only those whose inclinations are thoroughly dependable distinguish certainly what is lawful use from what is plundering, and what is dutiful defense from what is murder.

(*b*) Turning to situations that do comprise particular features of relevance: consensus may obtain among us because the data are common to all of us and because our inclinations, being alike, determine the same judgment when confronted by the same situation. This is what happens when a friend says to a friend, with no arguing and no attempt at logical connections, "I would have reacted as you did if I had been in the same situation." Here, consensus is obtained not by rational communication but by affective communion. Such consensus accounts for much friendly agreement among men. Notice, however, that if the problem is one of individual action, the emergence of a relevant particularity always may cause the closest friends no longer to see eye to eye. In a number of instances, the unique traits of my personality and of my history are decisively significant. Then my best friend would prove unreasonable if he told me "Under the same circumstances I would act differently." The relevant circumstances are not the same when they include individual variations—whether these pertain to innate constitution or to personal history.

(*c*) The problem is essentially different when the good to be achieved is common to all of us and calls for common action. But two cases must be carefully distinguished: either the good desired in common can be attained in a variety of ways, that is, through various forms of common action, or there is only one way to the common good. In the latter case, all members of the community, provided they are rightly inclined toward the common good and sufficiently aware of the data, react in the same way, and unanimity is ensured by affective communion—more precisely, by the common power of right inclination toward a good that is common to all. This is the most profound of the methods designed to ensure united action, and, no doubt, a community is in a weak condition when affective communion among its members no longer procures an approximation of unanimity in the hours of danger. But, again, it happens that several ways lead to the common good. It should even be said that when the acts of a community are considered with all their concrete modalities the common good always admits of being pursued in a variety of ways. Insofar as there is no unique determination of the way to the common good, affective communion, even under ideal conditions of good will and enlightenment, supplies no steady ground of unanimity. It is one of the essential functions of authority to procure the unity of common action when this cannot be guaranteed by affective communion—much less by rational communication.[18]

## Fulfillment and Explanation

We frequently experience the contrast between knowing enough to *do* what we have to do and knowing enough to *understand* why this is what we should do. This contrast is particularly noticeable when there is a question of acting in conformity to the orders of a superior. Orders may be so unclear as not to admit of certain fulfillment. But assuming that they are clear and complete enough to be carried out exactly, they may still fail to give the slightest hint of what their grounds may be. Having to fulfill orders without having a chance to achieve any degree or appearance of understanding is a condition that makes military life particularly uncongenial to some and congenial to others. Actually, in all phases of human existence fulfillment takes place under circumstances that do not make for unqualified understanding.

From the foregoing, it results, indeed, that the last practical judgment gives no explanation of what it commands. For instance, it is impossible to express intelligibly, that is, to explain, either to oneself or to someone else, with rigor and appropriateness, the ground of the decision to join a team of mountain climbers, here and now and under unique circumstances. Insofar as this discrepancy between what suffices for fulfillment and what is required for understanding is caused by contingency, we have to deal with an entirely normal state of affairs and we pay little attention to it. The plausible considerations involved in our deliberation seem to us perfectly sufficient, and we are willing to treat them as good explanations of our conduct; to be sure, they are satisfactory substitutes for explanations in a domain where explanation properly so called is unnecessary and impossible, just as by the preceding exposition (pp. 11–16) the probable ascertainment of the facts is a satisfactory substitute for theoretical certainty where such certainty is both unnecessary and impossible. Whether we obey the orders of a superior or act according to our own initiative, we are perfectly satisfied with a judgment that is determinate enough to be the right form of action and a final rule of fulfillment, even though it does not convey the final explanation of what has to be fulfilled.

Difficulties, perplexities, and the most harmful kind of revolt arise from the fact that the discrepancy between knowing enough to fulfill and knowing enough to understand is felt not only in the domain of contingency, where it is entirely normal, but also in an order of things where, if all were normal, intelligible clarity should obtain. Here, for the first time, we are moving away from this immediate form of action, this ultimate judgment, as practical as action itself, which has been the constant subject of our inquiry. But it is not possible to raise the issue of fulfillment versus explanation without reflecting somewhat on how this issue behaves in the field of moral essences, a field of intelligibility in which the philosopher would like to believe that he can explain the rules to be fulfilled.

This very difficult subject may be best approached by considering the part played in society by the men who possess the science of moral things. The Athenians were not interested in the epistemological status of ethical science. What concerned them was the influence of Socrates, especially on the youth. Let it be remarked, at this point, that a man possessed of a certain science, art, or expertness is normally and inevitably the object of two descriptions. He may be treated as the sheer bearer of a certain habitus, but under many circumstances he is considered as a social character, as a complex agent who, by reason of the habitus that he bears, is expected to discharge definite duties in society and to abide by rules of *human* use.

Thus, when we speak of medicine and physicians, we may refer either to the art of healing diseases and to the bearer of this art considered as such, or to the role that men trained in medicine must play in human and social relations. A physician taken as expert in medicine can be excellent without being a man of good character. He could let people die rather than answer night calls when he feels like resting. But if a physician is understood concretely as a person who has a role to play in the community of men, it is impossible for him to be excellent without being a man of high morality.

Indeed, the moral philosophers have, by reason of their capacities, definite functions to exercise among men. Let us pursue the comparison with the physician. Recommending a certain operation may involve a difficult moral problem. A family doctor who would be merely the bearer of an art would express himself in conditional terms and say something like this: "If and only if you want to recover health, the advisable thing is an operation whose likely consequences are such and such. But whether you want to recover health at this price is your business and not mine. Let me know your decision at your convenience." This conditional language is, in most cases, incompatible with the things that men and society expect of medical experts. Accordingly, a man possessed of excellence in the medical art, in order to practice his art in a way acceptable to society, must also be possessed of moral qualities and of good judgment; his patients want him to give them definite advice, not to utter merely conditional propositions. There is nothing wrong with a physician speaking *as a man* about things that pertain to medical practice. He often has to, inasmuch as he is committed to a social function. But abuse is perpetrated whenever advice of human, existential, and unconditional character is given in the name of the medical art, or of any art or science. Imagine the case of a statesman who under critical circumstances exposes himself to overwork and dangerous strain. The common good may demand that he be ready to sacrifice his life and it may, just as conceivably, demand that he should conserve his energy, albeit at the cost of poor management of important business by incompetent subordinates. This statesman's physician may be a person of moral excellence, a good and enlightened citizen; he may be well informed about what is going on, and perfectly qualified to give unconditional advice to his respected friend, the statesman. But the thing he cannot do is to contend that his advice is purely and simply medical. This would be a lie, for the medical art has nothing to say about the risks that citizens should or should not run in the service of the community.

Between the science of ethics and the ultimate practical judgment the relation is incomparably closer than between medicine and the human judgment of the medical man in the practice of his art. Yet the two cases are connected by an enlightening analogy inasmuch as in either case the unconditional pronouncement actually expected of the expert cannot proceed from expertness alone but presupposes moral virtues. If philosophers are asked about the justice of a particular war, all they can do, *qua* philosophers, is to recall the conditions to be satisfied for a war to be just. But people expect of them an unconditional and existential answer, referring definitely to this unique war. Are these people wrong? Not necessarily, for just as physicians, in order to fulfill their task in society, need to be men of good character, so we need to have among us philosophers and theologians who can be trusted with the application of their sciences to contingencies. In fact, some philosophers, and most of their listeners, would like to believe that philosophical expertness takes care of everything and that the last word about issues deeply involved in contingency can be uttered in a scientific capacity.

The role of the moralist in society contributes to confuse the issue of explanation in moral science itself. Like any scientific system, ethics is a rational discipline concerned with intelligible necessities. It falls short of its ideal, it purely and simply falls short of its nature, insofar as it is unable to unfold the intelligible necessity of moral essences.

This should be taken as well established: there exists a system of psychological illusions and social desires which incline the moral philosopher to underrate the restricting power of contingency and to overdo the possibilities of scientific accomplishment in moral affairs. Indeed, illusions that can be termed Socratic with some propriety, inasmuch as they express misplaced confidence in the ability of knowledge to solve the problems of action, have never ceased to haunt the conscience of enlightened societies. Surveying these illusions may remove the main obstacles to clear treatment of the relations between understanding and fulfillment.

(a) Socrates held, or at least suggested, that virtue is a science and can be taught. Accordingly, learning should supply a shortcut to good action. This intellectualistic optimism again assumed youthful naïveté in the eighteenth century, and in spite of many disillusionments it is still active in the mythology that often accompanies the theory of psychological, "behavioral," and social sciences. When an extremely crude illusion, which has been refuted many times, remains powerfully attractive, the important thing is not so much to refute it once more as to understand the sources of its success.

Obviously, the difficulties of virtue are so great that any of us is ready to welcome any device which would procure, at a lower cost and in a shorter time, the good conduct of many men.[19] Moreover, there certainly are cases in which we can honestly say that we would not have done wrong had we known what was right. Sometimes the only thing needed for the actual exercise of good action is better information about what should be done or avoided. But this happens only when good will is already present. Most babies are actually protected by simple rules of hygiene as soon as their mothers know what these rules are;

enlightenment here brings about the desirable action, so to speak, immediately, and we like to forget that the proper cause of righteousness in human action, viz., good will, virtuous will, was already there.

(b) Next comes the illusion that there is always a scientific way to answer the question "What ought I to do under the circumstances?" Many men have enough good will to keep away from the wrong, or at least from the worst, if they know definitely what is right and what is wrong and what is worst. Yet their will is not good enough to ensure the conditions of affective familiarity with the right and the wrong under obscure circumstances. These are the men who quiz moralists and complain about their disagreements. All too often, moralists take advantage of this "will to believe" on the part of their followers, and more or less unconsciously, they lose sight of the difference between what pertains to the science of ethics and what pertains to the virtue of prudence. This difference is often blurred in the area where the externals of scientific necessity are imitated by the striking generality of statements.

The science of ethics extends no further than the necessary connections by reason of which an act is one of justice or one of dishonesty, one of fortitude or one of cowardice, one of temperance or one of disorderly indulgence. At the other extreme, it is the privilege of prudence to deal with the singular and to answer unprecedented questions. Prudence is often defined by this privilege: this is perfectly fitting as long as we realize that answering general questions is also a proper function of prudence whenever, by reason of contingency, the general answer cannot be logically connected with any essential necessity. But at this point the psychological situation is almost inevitably obscure. When the answer of prudence is relative to strictly singular circumstances, it can be put in print without much danger of confusion: all understand that they are presented with a case history. On the contrary, when the question answered by prudence has a character of generality, its treatment normally assumes a systematic and doctrinal form which may, if we are not on our guard, deceptively imitate the ways of science. The proposition that it is dishonest to demand payment twice for one and the same thing, or to demand payment for a thing that does not exist,[20] refers to a moral essence and admits of scientific establishment. The proposition that, other things being equal, it is perfectly lawful to demand a compensation for a loss,[21] is also relative to an essence and is demonstratively established. On the other hand, any discussion of moneylending in contemporary society indispensably comprises prudential decisions. If these decisions hold in many cases, it is very helpful that they be printed and made readily available to all concerned. But many will naïvely believe that they are conclusions of moral science.

In order not to be misguided by the power of scholarly externals, we need to bear in mind that these conclusions, in spite of their generality, have been obtained not by logical connection, but by prudential determination. This implies that the author of the book, in order to be reliable, must be not only a learned person, but also a prudent one. John of St. Thomas has written that "a man may well be an ethical philosopher and theologian of great distinction and an imprudent sinner."[22] This statement would be objectionable if it referred to the factual exercise of philosophic and theological thought, for, regardless of logical necessities, a man of debased character is likely to be influenced by his evil inclinations. Thus, it is desirable, for *extrinsic* reasons, that the teacher of ethical science, whether philosopher or theologian, be possessed of sufficient virtue.[23] But John of St. Thomas is not speaking of concrete conditions and extrinsic factors; all he means is that in scientific ethics conclusions intrinsically depend on nothing else than rational connections with axiomatic principles. The science of ethics so understood does not comprise propositions whose generality is not guaranteed by essential necessity. Such propositions, no matter how general, cannot be ascertained without the intrinsic cooperation of virtuous inclination.

Let it also be recalled that a practical proposition that is general in character, but whose generality is not strictly connected with an essential necessity, may not hold in a number of cases. Furthermore, since it is normal for mores to change within certain limits, a case exceptional in one community may be common in another. Likewise, a practice almost always unacceptable in one generation may be commonly accepted in another; old-timers speak of decadence, yet the change may constitute progress. Failure to perceive the difference between the generality that is, and the generality that is not, strictly connected with essential necessity is harmful in more than one way. If we fancy that what generally holds under familiar circumstances necessarily derives from ethical natures, we render ourselves incapable of understanding the cases in which familiar rules of action actually do not hold. On the other hand, the diversity of the propositions that generally hold in different societies and generations often caused disbelief in the necessity of moral essences, and surrender to skepticism. The words of Pascal "Truth on this side of the Pyrenees, error on the other side" are ambiguous. (Pascal may be the first victim of their ambiguity.) It is perfectly normal that many rules of conduct which hold with overwhelming frequency on one side of the Pyrenees should hold only in rare cases on the other. But, on either side, lying is wrong, forging money is wrong, honoring one's parents is right, and helping the needy is right. These are ethical essences; if they are widely unrecognized on one side of the Pyrenees, or on both, all there is to be said is that even with regard to essential necessities the moral sense of men and of communities is apt to undergo setbacks.

(c) For all we know Socrates never held that no one is obligated unless he is given convincing reasons for the alleged obligation. Yet this can be described as a Socratic illusion, and the most threatening of all. So the Athenians felt. We often feel certain about right or wrong in a moral essence without being able to show clearly why it is right or wrong. Even in matters which admit of rational clarity, it often happens that available explanations are not airtight, and that there is a striking contrast between the firmness of our certainty and the vagueness of our explanation. Our intuitive acquaintance with the laws of the moral order is way ahead of our ability to connect moral essences with the first principles of morality, in other words, to show why an act is right or is wrong. *The system of natural law, before it is apprehended rationally, is known through affective connaturality.* It is normal and by all means desirable that this initial, non-explanatory knowledge be accompanied and strengthened, as soon as possible, by an understanding of the right and the wrong in specifically defined acts. But between the initial and the fully normal forms of our acquaintance with the right and the wrong the time discrepancy is indeterminate. The situation of moral understanding is analogous to that of the theoretical intellect. Many propositions have been firmly assented to long before they were demonstrated. The familiarity of the scientific mind with its object, the intellectual connaturality that the trained person enjoys in relation to an intelligible system, may determine an entirely safe assent to a proposition that no one has as yet succeeded in demonstrating. True, the same intellectual inclination which, at a time when a theorem is undemonstrated, already excludes the fear of error constitutes an urge toward perfect demonstration. But no law ever determined the amount of time between familiar acquaintance with and airtight proof of a certain theorem. Accordingly, we may expect generations and centuries to elapse between the achievement of affective connaturality and the understanding of the reasons why actions are right or wrong. It is even perfectly conceivable that mankind should end its career in this world without having clearly perceived, in all cases, the reasons why what we hold to be right is right and what we hold to be wrong is wrong.

Thus we have come to overestimate our factual accomplishments in the explaining of moral essences and to underrate the difficulties of understanding the things of morality, no matter how intelligible they may be in themselves. Apart from a long period of intoxication which apparently begins with Descartes, covers the eighteenth-century Enlightenment, and includes lasting trends in the nineteenth century, the notion of mystery in physical nature is altogether familiar and congenial. No one finds it surprising that a mathematician entitles a book *The Mysterious Universe*. Rather, we think ironically of the time when scientists did not find it ridiculous to declare that there are no more mysteries. It can truly be said, to the credit of twentieth-century philosophers and scientists, that they have restored a sense for mystery in the understanding of physical nature. Even the literary developments of our contemporaries on the meaninglessness and the absurdity of our experience sometimes can be interpreted as an expression—inadequate, indeed, and misleading—of a sense for mystery. Bearing all this in mind, let us ask the question: *Why should the moral universe be held less mysterious than the universe of physical nature?* As soon as this question is formulated, we sense how powerful the reasons are why mystery should not be less but be greater, and perhaps immensely greater, in the universe of morality than in the universe of nature, in ethics than in physics. Why should our science of moral things be less subject to a law of slow improvement, with many trials and errors, with many unsuccessful attempts at pointing out the real means of demonstration, than our explanation of things physical?

The trouble is that fulfillment must go on, while philosophers try and fail and achieve partial success and expound unconvincingly the few things that they have demonstrated. True, as soon as minds have conceived the ideal of an ethical science, that is, of a body of knowledge capable of showing—as far at least as universal essences are concerned—why this is said to be right and that is said to be wrong, and why the rules of fulfillment are such and such, the temptation is felt to refuse fulfillment until explanation is supplied. At least, there is a distinct danger that fulfillment be half-hearted, uncertain, and subject to reconsideration, as long as minds are not given cogent explanations. Beyond all historical incidents, this may be what the trial of Socrates perennially means. The Athenians seem to have thought that a keen interest in the understanding of ethical subjects causes perplexity and impairs the most indispensable resolutions. The traditionalistic movements which reacted against eighteenth-century rationalism, the Nietzschean protest, and some aspects of pragmatism express the conviction that rational analysis is, or may be, a threat to the firmness of action. Examples are at hand: the problems of justice are obscure enough; those concerning marriage, family life, and related subjects are incomparably more obscure.

It has been shown in the foregoing that when a question involves contingent occurrences, it absolutely cannot be answered by the ways of cognition, but only by those of inclination. In other words, the correct answer is obtained not by any logical connection with axiomatic premises but by the attractions and aversions of a soul in connaturality with the good. As to the questions that do not involve contingency but refer to essential necessities of the moral order, they admit of being answered either way. Inasmuch as we master the science of ethics, we are able to connect our answer logically with axiomatic premises, but whether we know scientific ethics or not, a dependable answer is obtained by inclination.[24] To be sure, the appropriate way of answering a question that does not involve contingency is the way of science and logical connection. But few men master the science of ethics to any extent, and what the most learned philosophers actually know is very little in comparison with what we would need to know if all major questions relative to moral essences were to be answered, without vagueness and uncertainty, according to the airtight methods that alone are explanatory. Fulfillment is not jeopardized, for, in order to fulfill, the ways of judgment by connaturality suffice, even though they be not the ways appropriate to the treatment of certain questions.

Is there anything abnormal about giving no answer, except that of connaturality, to a question regarding a moral essence? The notion of normality, in such a context, is ambiguous, for it admits of interpretation both in terms of essential necessity and in terms of human development. If essential necessity alone is being considered, the only normal state of affairs is the absolute perfection of all sciences, and it is abnormal, indeed, that a theorem of geometry be merely sensed to be true by the educated intuition of the geometrician. But it is normal that any perfection of man and of mankind, whether in the sciences or elsewhere, be achieved gradually, through a progress that is never unqualifiedly terminated. In such reference to human development, it is normal that a theorem be familiar to geometricians years or generations before it is demonstrated, and that questions relative to moral essences should not be firmly answered except by the inclinations of good and wise men.

But the danger that eagerness to explain may conflict with determination to fulfill can be taken care of by the understanding of fulfillment itself. It is true that in practical affairs what matters primarily is fulfillment, not understanding. It is true that whenever contingency is involved, the judgment that is fully sufficient as a rule of fulfillment can never be promoted to a condition of sufficiency as far as understanding is concerned. It is true that even in domains unaffected by contingency the poor development of our cognitions makes it factually impossible to give an explanatory account of many rules. And when all this is fully acknowledged, it remains a truth of essential significance that the kind of fulfillment that becomes rational agents always is itself, in some manner and degree, a rational thing. No matter how fortuitous the situations may be, and how unprecedented, unique, and unrenewable the relevant circumstances, I would not be fulfilling the rule of my action if there were not something rational about my way of fulfilling it.

Suppose that the right thing is done without thought, as a result of sheer habit. It is good, indeed, that the right thing should be done at all; this sort of fulfillment may be the best we can expect of feeble-minded persons who have been trained to do, out of habit, what their deficient constitution does not allow them to do according to more human modalities.[25] But, clearly, when the right thing is not done in the way proper to man, it is only in a material sense that we can speak of fulfillment. No matter how important it may be that the right thing be done at all, something essential to *human* fulfillment is lacking. Our best chance of getting the true signification of progress in moral philosophy, that is, in the explanation of moral essences, may well consist in considering rationality, understanding, and explanation as perfections that do matter for proper fulfillment in the life of rational agents. We shall not be looking for the demonstration of rules relative to contingent situations. And with regard to ethical essences we shall not hold that imperfection, no matter how shocking, in our power of explanation is an excuse for not fulfilling rules established in non-explanatory ways. We shall fulfill the demands of justice, such as they are perceived by the heart of the just, without waiting until philosophers have succeeded in explaining and demonstrating that such are, indeed, the rules of justice. And in incomparably more obscure domains, such as those of marriage and purity, we shall wholeheartedly fulfill the rules that we know to be right in spite of the difficulties that the best experts may not yet have managed in the airtight ways of explanation properly so called. But our action will be animated by an aspiration toward the most rational modalities of fulfillment. In such a vision of practical wisdom, moral philosophy no longer is the thing that threatens to cripple resolution and to endanger society. Rather, it is a constant effort, in a domain where unqualified intelligibility is *de jure* possible, to supply the whole system of our practical judgments with the rational modes that are required for the integrity of human fulfillment.

NOTES

1. Aristotle, *De anima* III, 10, 433A13; 11, 434A16. Cajetan, *In Summa theol.* I–II, 90, 1 ad 2.
2. Thomas Aquinas, *In Boeth. de Trin.* V, 1 ad 4.
3. Thomas Aquinas, *In III De anima*, 4, n. 635; *In I Eth.*, 3, n. 35; *Summa theol.* I, 14, 16; Cajetan, *In Summa theol.* I, 63, 3; John of St. Thomas, *Curs. phil.*, *Ars log.* I, *Sum.* 1, 3, ed. Reiser, 10B15 (*Outlines of Formal Logic*, trans. Francis C. Wade [Milwaukee: The Marquette University Press, 1955], p. 33); 2, 1, 4, ed. Reiser, 269B34 (*The Material Logic of John of St. Thomas: Basic Treatises*, trans. Yves R. Simon, John J. Glanville, and G. Donald Hollenhorst [Chicago: The University of Chicago Press, 1955], pp. 33–34).
4. Goethe, *Faust*, Part I, lines 1936–39.
5. Cf. the remarkable book of Isaiah Berlin on Tolstoy's view of history, *The Hedgehog and the Fox* (New York: Harper & Row, 1957).
6. Cf. Henri Bergson, *Time and Free Will*, trans. F. L. Pogson (New York: Harper & Row, 1928), chaps. 2 and 3; *Creative Evolution*, trans. Arthur Mitchell (New York: Holt, 1911), chap. 4; *The Creative Mind*, trans. Mabelle L. Andison (New York: Philosophical Library, 1946), Part II, chap. 4. The word "contemplative" is meant to express the determination to transcend all bias due to the requirements of action. There are important aspects of pragmatism in the philosophy of Bergson, but they are never allowed a character of ultimacy. What is ultimate is a disinterested intuition, related to contemplation indeed by its disinterestedness, but not purely cognitive, by no means motionless, and ready to animate the highest forms of action.
7. Ps.-Dionysius, *De divinis nominibus* 30 (PG III 729).
8. This is the point Peirce misses when he says that logic depends on ethics because ethics is the science of aims. See "The Essence of Mathematics," in *The World of Mathematics*, ed. James Ray Newman, 4 vols. (New York: Simon & Schuster, 1956), III 1782: ". . . the main reason why logic is unsettled is that thirteen different opinions are

current as to the true aim of the science. Now, this is not a logical difficulty but an ethical difficulty; for ethics is the science of aims." See also "A Syllabus of Certain Topics of Logic" (1903), *Collected Papers of Charles Sanders Peirce*, edd. Charles Hartshorne and Paul Weiss, 6 vols. (Cambridge: The Belknap Press of Harvard University Press, 1931–1935), I, para. 192: "Ethics . . . is the theory of self-controlled, or deliberate, conduct. Logic is the theory of self-controlled, or deliberate, thought; and, as such, must appeal to ethics for its principles." The aims of logic, say, valid and explanatory reasoning, involve no consideration of human use. There is such a thing as a logical, and such a thing as a non-logical use of reasoning, and logic tells me which is which. But it does not tell me whether I should write papers on logic, or write papers in demonstrative form about something else, or write essays that be persuasive rather than demonstrative, or just cultivate my garden: these are problems of human use with which ethics is concerned.

9. *On Free Choice* II, 19.

10. Aristotle, *Nicomachean Ethics* VI, 2, 1139A27; Thomas Aquinas, *In VI Eth.*, 2; *Summa theol.* I–II, 57, 5 ad 3; Cajetan, *In Summa theol.* I–II, 57, 5 ad 3.

11. It goes almost without saying that the unity of meaning of the word truth, as predicated of (1) the conformity of a judgment to a real state of affairs and (2) the conformity of a judgment to a right intention, is but one of analogy. The analogy of truth, as divided into theoretical and practical, is one of proper proportionality. It is in intrinsic fashion that both the theoretical and the practical judgment are true.

12. *Curs. theol.* I–II, d. 18, a. 4, ed. Vivès, VI, 638.

13. We are considering here not *introduction* to philosophy and to its various parts but philosophy itself, with the proper requirements of its demonstrative method. In the preliminary discipline which introduces the mind to the philosophic issues, inclination plays a part that is not only significant but also intrinsic; intrinsic, indeed, to the job of introducing to philosophy, and extrinsic to philosophy itself.

14. Just as sight symbolizes best the clear grasp of intelligible necessities, and touch the certainty of experimental knowledge, so smell symbolizes knowledge by inclination.

15. Aristotle, *Nicomachean Ethics* VI, 13, 1144Bff. Thomas Aquinas, *Summa theol.* I–II, 65.

16. G. Sorel, *Les Illusions du progrès*, 3rd ed. (Paris: Rivière, 1921), chap. 3, esp. pp. 162ff. The references to Condorcet's *Sketch of the Progress of the Human Mind* are most interesting.

17. "Among those statements which, despite their certainties, lack

the objective principle of intersubjectivity, the most typical are the prudential ones." Yves R. Simon, *Nature and Functions of Authority* (Milwaukee: The Marquette University Press, 1940), pp. 21ff. Also, "The prudence of the individual normally involves something singular and peculiar—it would almost be appropriate to say 'eccentric.' " Simon, *A General Theory of Authority* (Notre Dame: University of Notre Dame Press, 1962), p. 37. And "Because of the possible relevance of unique features in the determination of individual prudence, each man is threatened with the contingency of having to make his decisions in utter solitude and to act like no one else." Ibid., p. 38.

18. Yves R. Simon, *Philosophy of Democratic Government* (Chicago: The University of Chicago Press, 1951), pp. 29–31.

19. Suppose that a man trained in the contemplation of numbers and ideas reaches a state of absolute dedication to the good. Why not make a king out of this philosopher, and give him a chance to produce an enormous amount of sound action by directing the whole business of the city?

20. Thomas Aquinas, *Summa theol.* II–II, 78, 1.

21. Ibid. II–II, 78, 2 ad 1.

22. *Logic* II, q. 1, a. 4 (*Material Logic*, p. 46).

23. The case is no different from what it is in some parts of purely theoretical science. That debased morality should be accompanied by metaphysical excellence is not ruled out by any objective necessity, but it is made, in terms of fact, extremely improbable by the psychological relation between metaphysical truths, or some of them, and the dispositions of the human appetite.

24. Thomas Aquinas, *Summa theol.* I, 1, 6 ad 3.

25. It goes without saying that many actions are best performed out of sheer habit and that it is altogether good not to waste the freshness of our thought on things that habit takes care of best. In these cases we would not say that the rational way of fulfilling is absent, for the use of habit is itself contained in a rational planning of action.

# 2

# On Moral Philosophy

### Moral Science in Socrates and Aristotle

IN THE FIRST CHAPTER we considered the most determinate form of practical knowledge, a form of knowledge so completely faithful to its practical function that, in case of conflict, the requirements of direction always prevail over those of cognition. Aristotle's division of the intellectual virtues implies that conflicts can arise between the features proper to knowledge as such and those proper to knowledge as rule of action. Recall that for him the theoretical intellect is perfected by understanding, science, and wisdom; and the practical intellect, by art and prudence. Practical science is pledged to reconcile the opposite features of intelligible necessity and contingent determination.

Toward the end of the preceding chapter, we brought into focus the contrast between explanation and fulfillment. From the standpoint of action, fulfillment is the thing that principally matters. We noticed, however, that explanation is of relevance to fulfillment itself inasmuch as the rules governing a rational agent demand to be fulfilled in a rational manner. If it were possible for a man to behave irreproachably out of tradition and habit, with no understanding of what he is doing or of the reasons why he should act this way, the rules of human action would not be fulfilled except in a material sense; the rational form would be lacking. But prudence, the intellectual virtue that ensures the ultimate rule of fulfillment, adheres so closely to the contingencies of action that it cannot convey the intelligible necessities that make up explanation. At this point the function of moral science can be clearly described. In order for human affairs to be connected with the universe of intelligible necessity, we need a discipline in which the features of scientific thought unite with the purpose of directing action.[1]

It is commonly held that one philosopher did more than any other to arouse a scientific interest in the moral universe. A celebrated scene in the *Phaedo* tells how Socrates gave up inquiries into physical nature and dedicated his philosophy to the study of man.[2] Yet it is not easy to ascertain the meaning of the Socratic reformation. The Nietzschean picture of Socrates as an intellectual whose interest in rationality jeopardizes fulfillment and constantly threatens to kill "the native hue of resolution" is a product of dramatic craft, and its historical truth is not established. "Understanding kills action, for in order to act we require the veil of illusion. . . . What, both in the case of Hamlet and [in the case] of Dionysiac man, overbalances any motive leading to action, is not reflection but understanding, the apprehension of truth and its terror."[3] Another, and no less plausible, interpretation is suggested by these words of St. Augustine's: "Socrates is said to have been the first who directed the entire effort of philosophy to the correction and regulation of manners. . . ."[4] Thus, according to some, Socrates is primarily a man of knowledge: disappointed by the failures of the physicists, he carried out these new studies with a firm conviction that the world of human affairs was a subject truly proportionate to the ambitions and possibilities of the human intellect. Others see in him a man of action whose first concern is the improvement of men. If the latter interpretation is true, Socrates' notorious intellectualism, scoffed at in modern times by Nietzsche and a few others, would not be concerned with the glory and joy of knowing; it would be a theory relative to the causation of virtue. Socrates was, to say the least, strongly inclined to consider virtue as a science that could be taught and learned. He realized the difficulties of his paradox, and insofar as Plato's *Meno* can be treated as an historical document, it would seem that a time came when Socrates no longer believed that virtue could be taught. At all events, it can safely be asserted that for Socrates the knowledge and the ignorance of the right and the wrong play an all-important and often decisive part in the actual conduct of men. His main problem would not be one of explanation; it would concern the fulfillment of the rules formulated by the science of man. Socrates' conversion from physical nature to human affairs was not just an episode in the search of a scientific mind for a more rewarding field of intelligibility. It was, first of all, an act of dedication to the improvement of human manners.

In an essay that still deserves to be considered a classic, Emile Boutroux describes Socrates as the founder of moral science, and declares that the masterpiece of the scientific movement initiated by Socrates is the *Ethics* of Aristotle.[5] This prompts truly a fascinating question: In what sense, and to what extent, is Aristotle, the author of the *Ethics*, a follower of the Socratic reformation? To be sure, Aristotle is grateful to Socrates for having carried out, in the area of morality, a search for the universal which he holds to be the fundamental undertaking of the scientific mind.[6] Also, he appreciates the fact that in Socrates the theory of the universal is still free from the metaphysical constructs with which it will be associated in Plato.[7] On the other hand, Aristotle is deeply opposed to the intellectualistic tendencies of Socrates regarding the causation of virtue; no moralist is less inclined to believe that right action can be ensured by a merely cognitive process; his emphasis on the training of the appetitive powers sets him in sharp contrast to Socrates. Moreover, if Boutroux understands Socrates well, a Socratic science of ethics is not a science in Aristotle's sense; rather, it is a dialectical system, for, in lieu of axioms (i.e., premises possessed of rational evidence), it uses opinions commonly held among dependable persons. The *Ethics* of Aristotle would not be a Socratic accomplishment except when the philosopher fails to attain his own scientific ideal, fails to achieve a complete analysis of his subject into self-evident principles, and has to be satisfied with propositions generally held by people whose righteousness and experience are commonly acknowledged. Substituting a chapter of dialectic for a chapter of science is indeed an accident of great frequency in all areas of knowledge and at all times. This accident may be more frequent and less disquieting in ethics than elsewhere, for with regard to human actions men with no special training may be thoroughly trusted if they display qualities of good will, experience, and good judgment. No matter how profound the influence of Socrates upon Aristotle, we should not hesitate to say that the fundamental purpose of the science of ethics is not for Aristotle what it is for Socrates. According to Socrates, the role played by knowledge in the causation of righteousness is so great that whoever is concerned with improving the manners of men considers it the most urgent duty to promote a better knowledge of the right and the wrong and of the diverse virtues. For Aristotle, on the contrary, improved manners are the proper effect of an action exercised upon the desires of men by such methods as exhortation, inspiration, habituation, example, and coercion. But if such is the case, why is it good to write treatises on ethics? The answer seems to be unmistakable: besides anything that the science of ethics may do for the improvement of manners—perhaps indirectly, perhaps very slowly, and perhaps uncertainly—it is good to understand the world of morality just as it is good, at all events, to understand the world of nature or the world of mathematics. The ten books of Aristotle's *Ethics* contain many inquiries that it is good to have made, many principles that it is good to have formulated exactly, and many analyses that it is good to have performed, even if no improvement of men's behavior should actually follow from all that scientific work. In other words, the science of ethics, such as it is understood and carried out by Aristotle, possesses the excellence that belongs, regardless of what happens in the world of action, to the knowledge of that which is and to the explanatory certitude with which theoretical science gets hold of its object. No matter how significant its practical duties may be, moral philosophy contains an explanation of the things that make up the world of morality.

This may seem contrary to well-known passages of the *Nicomachean Ethics*. Aristotle briefly describes the qualities expected of people who take a course in moral science. He seems to be greatly concerned with keeping out poorly qualified auditors. Among these are youngsters; for lack of experience in human affairs, they cannot understand the subjects under discussion. Moreover, any person who is in the habit of following his passions should keep away from the lecture room of an ethics teacher. Even if passion did not prevent him from understanding, he would waste his time, and his study would be "vain and unprofitable, because the end is not knowledge but action."[8] This implies that the purpose of a course in ethics is to raise the moral level of the students. Such an interpretation seems to be at variance with the views generally held by Aristotle on the relation between science and action. For one thing, he does not expect knowledge to cause virtue. For another—as just recalled—the structure and content of his own writings seem to show that a course of ethics covers many things that it is good to know for the sake of their own truth. How, then, should these puzzling sentences be understood? Aristotle obviously wants certain people to stay out of his classroom; his concern is not purely epistemological. But his public, being familiar with Socratic ideas, is ready to consider that failure in human action amounts to failure in the undertakings of moral science. Thus, in order to get rid of obnoxious auditors, Aristotle appeals to views made popular by Socrates and his school; these views are not necessarily his own.

Yet it must be kept in mind that Aristotle, who is so far from expecting any theoretical operation to procure the rightness of action, is also very eager to mark under all circumstances the difference between the theoretical and the practical. If we want to put people on their guard against the illusion that theoretical processes may cause the virtuous regulation of our acts, we cannot be too particular about distinguishing the purpose of ethics from that of theoretical science. In the sentences described as "puzzling," Aristotle is concerned with the specificity of purposes. His opinion can be summed up as follows: if a student is interested in the knowledge of truth for its own sake, his place is not particularly in a course of ethical science. This is perfectly compatible with the view that a course of ethics should contain, and perhaps in great abundance, truths that are good to know for the sake of their own intelligibility. But if the intrinsic excellence of truth is what we are looking for, a course in theoretical science will answer our need more completely and more directly. There is, further, a distinct reason why Aristotle should consider with mistrust the purpose of seeking intelligibility in practical science. In often-quoted sentences, he remarks that the ethical sciences possess only in a low degree the scientific qualities of certainty and precision. Moral things admit of much variation, and in order that they not appear more definite than they actually are, it is often inevitable that they be treated merely in "rough outline." But if we are concerned with theoretical excellence, rough outlines are unsatisfactory ways of exposition, and we are tempted to do a thing that Aristotle dreads, viz., attribute to a science (here, ethics) a certainty and a precision of which it is not capable. By declaring that the purpose of practical science is not knowledge but action, Aristotle stresses what pertains to the practical sciences in unique fashion; at the same time, he takes precautions against the risk that practical science be treated according to requirements that do not belong to it. All this does not mean that Aristotle considers worthless the intelligibility procured by the science of ethics when it defines moral essences or demonstrates why some acts are right and some wrong. He certainly holds that human actions do not make up the most promising area for the mind in quest of theoretical truth; looking for theoretical perfection in an area distinguished by the pursuit of righteousness in action is likely to bring about misunderstanding and distortions. These concerns genuinely belong to the thought of Aristotle, but they are expressed in words that exaggeration renders somewhat inappropriate. If the understanding of essential necessities were not a significant purpose of practical science, prudence would supply all the rules needed for the direction of our acts. But, then, fulfillment would lack the character of rationality demanded by the nature of the moral agent. When Aristotle describes the good quality of action as the purpose of practical science and declares that the student in ethics has wasted his time if he has failed to achieve moral improvement, exaggerated expression makes it somewhat difficult to establish the real meaning and bearing of his remarks. Inasmuch as ethical science directs human action (albeit from a distance), it exercises a function that is entirely foreign to the theoretical sciences. For practical science failure in the direction of human acts means failure in its distinctive purpose. This does not imply that the science of ethics is expected, in Socratic fashion, to effect, with any regularity, the conversion of men to the ways of the good. The influence of ethical science on human action may be infrequent and it may be restricted, in many cases, to the rational mode of which we spoke in the foregoing.

## Moral Philosophy as a Theoretical Study

*Distinction of Moral Philosophy from Psychology*

*Know thyself*, the motto that Socrates learned from the oracle of Delphi, does not express any particular confidence in the possibilities of psychology. Let us not imagine that Socrates just shifted from one part of nature—say, the heavenly bodies—to another part of nature, namely, the human soul. The shift was much more radical. It carried thought from nature to morality and from a predominant interest in knowledge to a predominant, if not exclusive, interest in the improvement of men through methods that are, indeed, intellectual and scientific. The first treatise in psychology is Aristotle's *On the Soul*; it has always been considered a part of natural philosophy, and never was held to be connected with ethics in any particular fashion. Aristotle's psychology is the altogether theoretical science of living things. Although it studies the powers that elicit moral actions, it is not in any sense a study of morality. The three books of the treatise *On the Soul* contain many expositions with which the moral philosopher should be familiar (theories of the sense appetite, of the understanding, and of the rational desire); these are physical expositions, but to understand the world of morality, it is necessary to know the natures they are concerned with. When we advise a beginner in moral philosophy to study some psychological issues thoroughly, we do not imply that there is any epistemological unity between ethics and the physics of the soul. By declaring that a certain subject is a necessary preparation to the study of another subject, we answer a purely pedagogical question. In the ethical writings of Aristotle there is an abundance of psychological remarks and expositions, but this fact is of no epistemological significance. It simply means that an exponent of scientific disciplines occasionally treats a subject, not at the place that epistemological relations would indicate, but at the place that is pedagogically the most convenient.

For instance, the study of the will, which belongs to psychology insofar as the will is a certain nature, is also of obvious relevance for the moral philosopher insofar as voluntary actions are the matter of morality. If epistemological requirements alone were to be taken into consideration, the moral philosopher, who is responsible for a treatise on the matter and the form of morality, would leave out all subjects pertaining to the nature of the will. But in the management of such an issue as that of the matter and the form of morality, it is indispensable to have at hand a number of considerations properly relative to the will as a nature. In fact, if we want to know Aristotle's psychology of the will, we cannot be satisfied with the three books of *On the Soul*; we have much to learn from the *Ethics*.

In our time the situation is more complex because psychology has confusedly developed in several directions. About two generations ago, a writer whose name I do not recall suggested that we should speak of psychologies in the plural. We are now ready to take seriously what was meant to be no more than a provocative joke. Indeed, the disciplines today designated by the word psychology lack epistemological unity. Academic programs and syllabi, in spite of much confusing uncertainty, seem to assume, except where strict positivism prevails, that there are two sciences of the soul, one of which is akin to philosophy, and the other to the positive science of nature. To teach the first, academic authorities will select a man of philosophical training who has read Plato, Aristotle, Lucretius, Descartes, Leibniz, John Stuart Mill, and William James. To teach the second, they will prefer a man who has spent some time in psychology laboratories and in centers for the study of nervous diseases. Terminology is changing and confused. Metaphysical psychology, rational psychology, speculative psychology, philosophy of the mind are the expressions most often used to designate this ill-defined science of the soul which is commonly held to be the business of the philosophers. Let us call it philosophic psychology.

Throughout the nineteenth century, psychologists were divided concerning the possibility of a philosophic science of psychological phenomena. Wherever positivism obtained, psychology was held to have reached the condition of independence which befits sciences in their maturity. Other schools of thought, generally characterized as spiritualistic, held that, by reason of its subject, the science of the soul was bound to maintain a particularly close connection with philosophy. To be sure, all questions pertaining to the relation between the empiriological[9] and the philosophic standpoints in the study of nature involve great difficulties. It often is impossible to determine the line between what pertains to the philosophy of nature and what pertains to the empiriological science. According to the spiritualists (for the most part Scottish or French), distinguishing between empiriological expressions is not only more difficult but also less desirable when the facts under consideration are psychological. It seems reasonable to say that in our time the situation is characterized by the joint operation of two tendencies. On the one hand, it is more and more generally held that the development of a non-philosophical interpretation should normally extend to all parts of the physical world. On the other, the demand for a sharp separation between philosophy and positive science is not so resolute as it used to be in the recent past. Several physicists or biologists of this century are commonly regarded as men of great significance in the philosophy of nature. Concerning the problem of moral philosophy, the really important distinction is not that between science and philosophy, but that between theoretical and practical science. Let us, accordingly, pose the following question: Whether it is considered a positive science akin to the other disciplines commonly designated as the sciences, or a branch of philosophy, is psychology interpreted as a mere theory of the psychological facts, or is it granted the power to direct in some way the actions of man? In this respect, there are significant differences between the best-known tendencies of the nineteenth century and those of our time. The spiritualistic ways of thought which tended to identify psychology and philosophy also tended to identify psychology—interpreted philosophically—and ethics. In our time, the situation has been greatly changed by the development of several arts founded upon empiriological psychology. We are touching upon an issue that makes for disastrous confusion, and no precaution should be spared to ensure clarity. Let it be recalled, first of all, that there are two ways for thought to be practical. Prudence and moral science belong to the same genus of practical thought, yet they do not achieve the same degree of practicality, and it should be said that, within the unity of a genus, they have diverse ways of being practical. Arts and techniques belong to another genus of practical thought. Within this genus also there are various degrees of practicality, but the most significant part of the theory is that the genus that comprises art is a genus less practical than the genus that comprises prudence. Recall that in Aristotle the fundamental division of cognition is tripartite: a cognition that is not purely theoretical may be concerned either with things to be made, and then Aristotle speaks of *productive* knowledge; or with human actions precisely considered as human, and here Aristotle speaks of practical knowledge (whether scientific or prudential). Theoretical science, on the other hand, has as its purpose the perfection of knowledge, not the direction of action. Many like to think that theoretical science is of great importance for the successful direction of action, that crafts and techniques deteriorate if studies do not make large enough the place given to disinterested and purely theoretical research. These remarks are true, but have no relation to the constitution of theoretical science. They relate to considerations of a psychological or pedagogical character and not to the theory of a scientific object as such. For every theoretical science, the state of perfection consists in explanatory knowledge, or, more exactly, in the certainty of its explanations. The question "What are the things?" is answered perfectly when we have understood the relation of the things to their causes and principles—understood, that is to say, perceived their intelligible necessity.

When the moral philosopher effects the basic work of defining, in Socratic fashion, such moral essences as fortitude or temperance, he certainly tries to know, in a particular field, what the things are. His undertaking remains, to a large extent, a theoretical one. He is looking for essences, *logoi*, formulas of intelligible necessity which ground demonstrative and explanatory knowledge. In his case as well as in that of the physicist, it can be said that a state of perfection is attained when things are known in and through their intelligible relation to their causes and principles. Moral philosophy, then, is, *in some basic way*, a theoretical science.

*Human Use and the Distinction of Theoretical from Practical Science*

But moral philosophy does something that no purely theoretical science does. It is concerned with problems of right and wrong use. What does it mean to make use of a thing? It means to apply it to an operation. Let us recall our discussion of use in Chapter 1 (pp. 9–11). There we made the all-important distinction between perfection of nature and perfection of *human* use, between use in relation to some particular end and use in relation to the perfection of man as a voluntary and free agent. That contrast is of the greatest significance for the understanding of *moral* knowledge in its concern for perfection of nature and perfection of *moral* use. Generally speaking, perfection of nature and perfection of human use are independent of each other. It is possible to make a good use of a thing in poor physical shape, and a good use of a thing in excellent shape, although we should remember that the good or bad shape of a thing may determine an inclination toward right or wrong use. The use of a car is less likely to be good if the condition of the brakes is poor, so that determination to make a good use of his car inclines a man to decide that the brakes will be repaired as soon as possible. Correspondingly, a weak will is a nature in poor physical condition. It is possible to make a good use of a weak will, but whoever is determined to make a good use of his will does his best to strengthen it. *It is mostly when the nature under consideration is an appetite that the perfection of nature matters for the perfection of use.* The sense appetite is capable of unsound conditions which, indeed, pertain to nature, not to use, but are of such character that no good use can be made of the inclinations that they determine.

Let us consider the effects of the consideration of use on the epistemological character of a discipline. Corresponding to our definition of theoretical science (as involving the question "What are the things?"), let it be said that the practical question is "What ought we to do?" Secondary to it, such questions as

"What should we have done?" or "What is it that should have been done under the circumstances?" can be listed as practical questions. If we suppose that a discipline is intrinsically concerned with the consideration of the right and the wrong use, we may say that this consideration is intrinsically practical and that it suffices to make the discipline practical in an intrinsic sense. A discipline would be practical in an extrinsic and accidental sense when it happened to be used for the purposes of action, as in the case of a practical-minded engineer who would not study geometry if this theoretical discipline were not necessary to a man who plans to build bridges. In this case, geometry has not become practical in any but an extrinsic and accidental sense. Obviously, when Socrates looks for the definition of temperance or fortitude, the practical question "What ought we to do?" pertains to his research intrinsically. Let this point be clear: the consideration of the right and wrong in use suffices to render a discipline practical in an intrinsic, essential, and proper sense.[10]

## Use and the Two Ways of Practical Synthesis

We saw in the preceding chapter that the considerations designed to answer practical questions take on a synthetic character in sharp contrast with the analytical method used to answer theoretical questions. Moreover, a judgment that is unqualifiedly practical, as practical as action itself, implies an approach that is synthetic, in two respects. (*a*) For one thing, this judgment puts together, in the form of a command, a certain thing to be done and the act of existing. This we have called the *synthesis of realization*. Theoretical sciences may effect various syntheses; but this one, the synthesis of realization, is entirely foreign to them and belongs exclusively to the practical order. (*b*) Secondly, the thing to be done is supposed to be complete, to comprise every circumstance necessary for that thing to be good here and now. Some of these circumstances may be relative to the contingencies of the situation. In contrast with these synthetic ways of practical thought, theoretical thought is analytical. We saw in Chapter 1 that analysis is not synonymous with decomposition, that it signifies primarily the act of tracing an effect to its cause and a consequence to its principle. The cause and the principle may have the character of wholes. It is only when they have the character of parts that scientific analysis consists in decomposition.

In many instances, however, the process of tracing an effect to its cause presupposes the decomposition of an accidental whole into the essential components that make it up. When the question is "What ought we to do? What are we going to do?" accidental wholes are always involved. If no accidental wholes were involved, the answer to the practical question would perhaps be incomplete. Obviously contingent circumstances may always be of relevance for the purposes of action. If they are not considered, the practical question may be incompletely answered. The answer would remain at a distance from total practicality.

Moral philosophy does not pretend to be totally practical. Nor could it be without dealing with contingencies that are so many restrictions on intelligibility. The primary purpose of moral philosophy is to understand moral essences. This implies that the said essences are abstracted from, pulled out of, the contingent aggregates in which they are generally engaged in immediate experience. Thus, insofar as analysis means explanation, i.e., the tracing of an effect to its proper cause, moral philosophy is analytical. And insofar as analysis means the decomposition of an accidental whole into the essences that make it up, again, moral philosophy is analytical.

Let us now ask whether moral philosophy retains in any way the synthetic procedures that characterize practical thought. In Chapter 1, when practical thought was considered at the peak of its practicality, we said that the synthesis of a certain "this" and the act of existing essentially pertains to it. Now, from the very fact that moral philosophy is concerned with use, it is concerned with this synthesis. To say that such and such a use of our powers is right is to say that such and such a use must come to exist, must be united with the act of existence under the proper circumstances. To say that fortitude is a virtue is to say, among other things, that one must *be* courageous, that fortitude must be united with the act of existence. To say that stealing is wrong is to say that this particular essence, stealing, should not be united with the act of existing. Thus, as far as the synthesis of a certain "this" and the act of existing is concerned, moral philosophy involves the synthetic way characteristic of practical thought. Yet this seems to be entirely the same as saying that moral philosophy aims at directing action. Let us notice again that, of all syntheses, the synthesis of realization seems to be the only one that belongs exclusively to practical thought. Are we saying that, in this respect, viz., as far as the synthesis of "this" and "to be" is concerned, the synthetic character of practical thought is unqualified? Rather, it is a synthesis of another type, practical in a proper sense, and yet, in accordance with its own level of intelligibility and abstraction, determined by and following upon the synthesis of realization. In this way the synthesis is qualified, but it is important to determine the origin of the qualification. This origin does not lie in the relation of the "this" to "to be," but in the conditions required for the building of the "this." The "this" to be brought into existence cannot be built without the contingencies that are excluded by the primary purpose of moral philosophy, which is the understanding, the explanation, of moral essences.

We can now approximate the sense in which moral philosophy can be said to *direct* human action. By the very fact that it is concerned with the right and the wrong use of our powers, moral philosophy says that human action ought to be such and such. And this is an act of direction. However, direction is obviously incomplete when the action to be elicited is considered apart from the contingencies that are a part of it when the "this" under consideration is joined with the act of existing. To say that moral philosophy directs human action *from a distance* is to use a well-grounded metaphor. In fact, the distance is often great. We are aware of it when, having settled an issue of moral philosophy, we realize that we still have to perform a long inquiry to reach a prudential answer.

Philosophers who write on social and political subjects are particularly aware of this situation. Their listeners do not allow them to stop where the methods of philosophy have their possibilities. These people, impatient and without respect for epistemological borderlines, want the philosopher to give them a concrete answer, an answer holding here and now, an answer as inclusive as possible of considerations for the here and the now. If it is suggested that the man who is well qualified to treat a question philosophically may not be qualified to treat its prudential aspects, they do not understand, and they may even want their money back. To pacify them, the philosopher has to acquire, if he can, a practical habitus. Just gathering the data is an enormous job which makes one feel how large the distance is between philosophy and a consideration inclusive of prudence. But a new difficulty arises: these people want to believe that the very ultimate conclusions are philosophically established, which is a lie. This lie, this impossibility of a necessary connection between the philosophical and the prudential, is another and the most decisive sign of the distance between the last word of philosophy and the words of prudence.

## Moral Philosophy as Theoretically Practical Science

Lastly, what kind of truth belongs to moral philosophy? The synthetic character of the practical judgment, with regard to the act to be elicited and in general the things to be brought into existence, is determined by a law of fulfillment that is basically the same as the law of integrity, which is a metaphysical law of the good (the law of Dionysius). As shown above, there may be a contrast; there is, indeed, at least a relative contrast between the law of fulfillment and the law of explanation. In order for the law of the good to be fulfilled, the most contingent circumstances ought to be considered. This eagerness to include the most contingent runs directly contrary to the law of explanation, for, once more, to explain is to analyze an effect into its essential cause, a consequence into its essential principles. Accidental causes and principles, which concern fulfillment in intrinsic fashion, just interfere with the process of explanation. Thus, to understand the character of moral philosophy in light of the basic contrast between synthesis and analysis, we must ask whether moral philosophy is basically designed to ensure a fulfillment or to procure an explanation. If the question is so stated, the answer is obvious. We may, without philosophy, be satisfied with the way laws are fulfilled. Things may be done the way they should be done as an effect of virtue and prudence.

Under these happy circumstances we still find it necessary to philosophize. It is true that, all things being equal, philosophy procures a better mode of fulfillment, but this is not the problem. The problem is for us to understand why we are supposed to act the way we do. Assuming a state of ideal completeness in fulfillment, we still would want to understand why such and such laws ought to be fulfilled, and it is precisely for the sake of such understanding, for the sake of explanation, that, even without hoping for more complete fulfillment, we want to philosophize. It is entirely clear that the primary purpose of ethical philosophy is not fulfillment but explanation. From this it follows that moral philosophy is principally analytical.

Take the definition of virtue according to Aristotle, St. Augustine, and St. Thomas. The author of the book *The Imitation of Christ*, who is probably concerned more with fulfillment than with explanation, proclaims somewhere "What good will it do you to be able to argue about the Blessed Trinity if, through pride, you displease the Blessed Trinity?" In the same spirit one might say that the significant thing is to have virtue and not to be able to define it. Indeed, in terms of fulfillment, virtue is the significant thing. If the definition of virtue is significant, it is not so much with regard to fulfillment as with regard to understanding and explanation. The expression "not so much . . . as" must be understood literally. We are not saying that definition, understanding, and explanation are, with regard to fulfillment, devoid of significance, but only that they are not so significant as virtue itself. Let us examine the method of definition typically found in a work of moral philosophy. Virtue is an active quality; more precisely, it is an active habitus, that is, an active disposition whose stability is guaranteed by an essential and objective necessity. This habitus renders the human subject good not in a particular respect, as in the case of a science or a technique, but absolutely speaking or, what amounts to the same thing, as man. The rectitude procured by virtue is not that of a particular action, but, in the most appropriate sense, that of human life. "Virtue is that by which we live rightly."[11] Most of all, virtue is distinguished from the other good active habitus by the property of procuring not only the good quality of the act, but also the good use of the ability to act. A skilled shoemaker will make good shoes if he pleases, but he may not please and yet remain good as a shoemaker. Of the just, on the contrary, it cannot be said that he will pay his debt exactly and on schedule if he pleases; inasmuch as he is just, he certainly pleases to do whatever justice demands. Whereas it is always possible to make a wrong use of such good qualities as sciences and arts, to make a wrong use of virtue is contradictory. As Aquinas shows, this definition explains virtue in terms of its four causes: the analytical method, which characterizes works of thought primarily in relation to explanation, is unmistakably at work here. The ways of a discipline that treats ethical subjects as Aristotle, Augustine, and Aquinas treat the subject of virtue are theoretical. No matter how practical it may be in other respects, moral philosophy is a theoretical science as far as its fundamental ways are concerned. Its own way of being practical is a theoretical one. It is a *theoretically practical science*. These considerations should settle the question of the kind of truth that belongs to the propositions of moral philosophy. We distinguished above between the theoretical truth of a proposition, its truth unqualifiedly so called, i.e., its agreement with the real state of affairs, and its practical truth, i.e., its agreement with a right desire. We saw that the principal truth of the prudential judgment, the truth that belongs to it properly as a practical and prudential judgment, and alone admits of being established with certainty, is practical truth. This agrees with the primacy of fulfillment in prudence.

## Moral Philosophy as Intrinsically Practical

*The Synthesis of Nature and Use*

After this discussion of the explanatory, and, accordingly, analytical character of moral philosophy, it can be wondered whether moral philosophy retains the character of a practical science in an intrinsic way. The proof that moral philosophy, understood in Aristotle's sense, is not a part of natural philosophy but a practical science in a proper sense derives from the fact that moral philosophy considers problems of use, whose consideration is totally foreign to theoretical science. The behavior of psychology is, in this respect, clearly indicative. Whether the psychologist who studies, for instance, memory, follows the ways of philosophy or those of positive science, he is always and exclusively concerned with the laws expressing the nature of memory. If he ever indulges in considerations about how man should use his memory in order to be good and happy, to serve society, and to save his soul, any reader would know that the scientific perspective has changed and that the gentleman whom we knew and esteemed as a psychologist is now speaking in the capacity of moralist—a capacity in which we might question his excellence. The scientific perspective changes radically when, not satisfied with the consideration of natures and their explanation—i.e., the tracing of effects to the natures that account for them—the scientist or the philosopher brings in the consideration of use, when, that is, he is no longer satisfied with the *isolated* consideration of nature but effects the *synthesis* of nature and use, and points to the synthesis of realization.

With regard to the contrast of analysis and synthesis as basic expressions of the theoretical and the practical ways, let it be said that the first and indispensable synthesis distinguishing the practical from the theoretical is the putting together of nature and use. Prior to this synthesis it is impossible to speak of practical thought except in an improper, accidental, and subjective way—as if we say that geometry is, for a particular student, an altogether practical subject, meaning thereby that he is interested only insofar as acquaintance with geometry leads to diplomas and positions. But as soon as the particular synthesis constituted by the putting together of nature and use is essential, science is practical in an intrinsic way.

It is striking that such a faithful Aristotelian as John of St. Thomas holds that moral philosophy, unless it includes prudence, is a purely theoretical science, a part of the philosophy of nature, a psychology of virtues. What he means when he speaks of moral philosophy with and without prudence can be interpreted as follows. In a treatise of moral philosophy we almost always find propositions that cannot be deductively connected with the principles because they involve in essential fashion the consideration of contingent circumstances. When the connection with the principles is not logical and deductive, it cannot be anything other than prudential. Suppose that a philosopher, after having explained the foundations of the right of private ownership, and shown that this right calls for limitations, undertakes to show what those limitations should generally be in the nations and in the period in which the book is likely to be read; since the desirable limitations of the right of private ownership essentially depend on historical circumstances, the connection between judgments on these limitations and the principles of moral philosophy cannot be of the logical type. It has to be effected, not by certain rules and determinate ways, but by rules of good judgment, contingent and prudential rules. Clearly, no matter how sound the treatment of the essence of the right of property may be, the advice given by the philosopher to the legislator regarding the limitations of the right of property in a particular society is no better than his prudence. John of St. Thomas considers practical the work of the moral philosopher who does not stop at the point where the power of logical connections is exhausted, but supplements the power of deduction with that of prudential connection. Clearly, a treatise comprising, over and above whatever can be done by logical connection, a system of prudential considerations is an accidental whole, the frequency of the accident being well accounted for by the eagerness of the reader. To be sure, few readers are satisfied with a philosophic exposition of ethical matters that stops where the power of deduction is exhausted, that is, at a great distance from action.

In the light of a familiar acquaintance with the work of Aristotle, these views of John of St. Thomas' are paradoxical and can hardly be accounted for save by an accident whose exact nature we shall never know but can reasonably guess. There was perhaps, in the classroom next to his, an ambitious philosopher who told his students that they would come to possess the last word of practical wisdom just by taking his course, or who claimed to answer definitely prudential questions in consultations authoritatively given in the capacity of philosopher or of theologian. Such abuse is indeed common among theologians; it would be no less common among philosophers if their advice were taken seriously in the problems of action.

Good theologians can work out the principles involved in a given case—assuming that they are honest—but to recognize the principles in the case, and accordingly to determine what principles are at work in this particular case, could not be done by the theological habitus. A prejudiced theologian, blinded by his political passions or the ideology prevalent in his family circle, would be less of a witness, in such a case, than a common man with ordinary instruction. Even a man as serene as John of St. Thomas may have been so irritated by philosophic imperialism as to underrate the practical meaning of moral philosophy and overdo its theoretical character. Such an hypothesis alone could account for the fact that he could write that the *Ethics* of Aristotle is a chapter of natural philosophy. Again, in the light of a familiar acquaintance with the works of Aristotle, it is absolutely clear that the *Ethics* belongs to an entirely distinct domain, and it can safely be said that the division of philosophy into logic, physics, and ethics, which became current in the post-Aristotelian period, is well-grounded in the work of Aristotle. What we are doing here is pointing to the indicative, the suggestive, value of a familiar acquaintance with the physiognomy of works of thought. Such indications have no demonstrative value, of course, but as indications and suggestions, they cannot be neglected.

In our discussion of the ultimately practical judgment, we described the unique relation of this judgment to human use. It is important to specify, with all possible accuracy, the way in which moral philosophy is related to human use. The question can be specified as follows: Is human use a pure object for moral philosophy, or is it already—by already, I mean, in spite of the theoretical, analytical, explanatory mode of moral philosophy—an end? A pure object is a pure formal cause; it is concerned with the difference between the same and the other, and it may be concerned with the essential conditions of effectuation, but it has nothing to do with effectuation itself. If use were a pure object for moral philosophy, the judgment of moral philosophy would have no intrinsic and direct tendency to be the form of action. So the proposition that use is not a pure object for moral philosophy can be proved by the proposition that moral philosophy aims at the direction of action, if this latter proposition is already granted. But a more profound problem should be examined, at bottom the very problem that we shall be considering throughout our discussion of the freedom from value-judgments in social science (see below, Chapter 4). Recall the words of Maritain: "There is a theoretical science of the nature of free choice, but of the use of free choice there can be only a practical science." A science of use devoid of any tendency toward the effectuation of what is right would not be moral philosophy. Further, it seems that it would not be possible at all. The case will be settled if we can show that the consideration of use is necessarily that of an object actually exercising the capacity of end. Of course, it is possible to study the notion of use in an entirely theoretical fashion. Thus in the decomposition of the volitional process into twelve phases,[12] there is no difference in epistemological status between the consideration of the first four phases and of the fifth—use of the reason to deliberate—or between the first nine and the last two, on the one hand, and, on the other, the ninth one, which is the use of all our powers and instruments in the execution of our designs. It is decisively important to specify just what angle of consideration, just what degree of concreteness, relates the consideration of use to the effectuation of the right use, gives use the character of an end over and above that of an object, causes the consideration to be practical and to pertain to moral philosophy.

## The Antecedence of Judgment

The essential character of the consideration of use in moral philosophy entails a logical and epistemological feature of utmost significance. In moral philosophy, as well as in any way of thinking that is practical in a proper sense, *judgment enjoys priority over concept*. But in order that the meaning of this proposition be clear, an approach both doctrinal and historical is necessary. Insofar as such generalizations are ever permissible, it can be said that philosophers commonly hold that judgment enjoys priority over concept in terms of perfection and finality. It is quite obvious that the mind that apprehends a meaning or essence without having anything to say about it is still in an initial phase of its activity. The issue on which philosophers are significantly divided is the relation of priority and posteriority between concept and judgment in the order of intelligible dependence. Let it be said that the question amounts to whether the concept is presupposed by the intelligibility of the judgment or the judgment by that of the concept. But the meaning of this question can hardly be specified without a glance at its history.

In Plato the apprehension of an intelligible object, of an idea, is purely and simply anterior to any judgment about the properties of this idea or its relations to other ideas. As known, the apprehension of ideas, in the philosophy of Plato, results from a conversion to a world of intelligible forms. If the theory of reminiscence is understood as the sheer expression of factual truth, the world of intelligible forms has been contemplated in a previous life, prior to the catastrophe that cast souls into bodies like prisoners into jails. If the theory of reminiscence is interpreted as a myth, then it means that, without our being able to explain why things are as they are, everything takes place in intellectual life *as if* our intelligible apprehensions were not in any way derived from sense experience, but altogether from an intelligible experience antecedent to our present struggle toward the understanding of things. In either case the conversion that leads to the apprehension of intelligible forms is accompanied by an aversion to the world of sense experience, which is held to be hopelessly deceptive. In Aristotle and his school, the order of the operations of the mind is unmistakable: first comes the apprehension of essences, then the enunciative and judicative synthesis, then the discourse of reason, itself aimed at the establishment of new judgments. The apprehension of the intelligible essences and the concept, which expresses both the form apprehended and its apprehension, result from an abstraction exercised on the data of sense experience. All attitude of aversion to the sensible world has disappeared, for it is sense experience which, through its regularities, makes it possible for the intellect to circumscribe and to apprehend essences, no matter how inexhaustively.

In spite of divergences that appear more and more profound as our knowledge of the history of thought improves (Descartes did not see much difference between Plato and Aristotle), Aristotle remains a Platonist on these two all-important points: (1) like Plato, he holds that there is an infinite qualitative distance between any sensible and any intelligible object. Like Plato, he holds that intelligent cognition cannot be brought about by a mere evolution of sense cognition, but requires a cause proportionate to its distinctness and its loftiness; this cause is the active intellect, on which Aristotle wrote only a few lines. The vehemence of the controversies centered in these few words of Aristotle's[13] shows that during the scholastic centuries many understood the meaning and significance of Aristotelian problems, even though they may have often misunderstood the answer of Aristotle. (2) Like Plato, Aristotle considers that judgment is a cognition of the truth about things that have already been intellectually apprehended.

In the philosophy of Kant the opposition between the rational and the empirical is as sharp as it is in Plato, and this opposition is as fundamental a feature of Kantianism as it is of Platonism. But it is an equally fundamental feature of the philosophy of Kant that every vision, every intuition, every *Anschauung*, every apprehension of content, is the work of sense experience and that, no matter what elaboration it may undergo, it remains unqualifiedly empirical. The philosophy of Kant admits of no intellectual apprehension, whether of the intuitive or of the abstractive description. This philosophy excludes all contemplation of ideas by way of Platonic conversion and it no less certainly excludes any abstraction in the sense of Aristotle, that is, the disengagement of an intelligible content from the data of sense experience. When these two features of Kantianism, the irreducibility of the rational and the exclusion of all intelligible apprehension, are firmly grasped, it is easy to see that rational activity, in Kant, is primarily connective, synthetic, judicative, dedicated to the putting together of data that experience leaves scattered, unordered, unscientific, in short, empirical. Kant overcame the skepticism of Hume and rationally vindicated Newtonian science by placing in the mind the principle of the necessary connections and the rational orderliness that are the characteristics of the scientific universe and cause the joy of scientific intelligence. The interpretation of Kantianism as a subjectivistic philosophy is tenable indeed from some standpoints, but not from the standpoint of Kant himself, for the scientific object, according to his philosophy, is constituted as scientific object by the connective and judicative activity of the mind. It is from the mind's contribution that it derives its character of scientific objectivity. If cause and effect, for instance, are so connected as to find place in scientific orderliness, it is not because of a necessity intelligibly perceived in the ontological constitution of things; on this, Kant agrees with the conclusions of Hume. But he does not, like the skeptic Hume, reduce the firmness of causal connections to the subjective stability of a habit. There is something objective, in the most deeply Kantian sense, in the steady connection of cause and effect. The judicative activity that connects phenomena in orderly systems of effects and causes is what confers upon the data of sense experience the character and dignity of scientific objects. But the judicative activities of the intellect are themselves contained in a system of concepts, viz., quantity, quality, relation, and modality. Quantity comprises unity, plurality, and totality; quality comprises reality, negation, and limitation; relation comprises substance, cause, and community; and modality comprises possibility, existence, and necessity. These are the concepts of the understanding, such as Kant defines them. They are posterior to, and determined by, systems of judgments: the concept of unity corresponds to the universal judgment; the concept of plurality, to the particular judgment; the concept of totality, to the singular judgment; etc. True, Kant speaks also of empirical concepts, but this is no more than a concession to the language of his time. The abstraction that brings about the so-called empirical concepts involves no metaphysical transmutation; it is just the constitution of a common image by elimination of individual particularities as it was described by the sensationist psychologists of the eighteenth century. Whenever the term concept, in Kant, conveys the irreducibility of the rational, it designates a form of judicative activity determined by and posterior to the laws of the diverse kinds of judgments.

The obscurities of the philosophy of Kant were not an important obstacle to its influence, for the obstacle that they constituted was easily swept away by the extraordinarily powerful historical forces present in the philosophy of Kant. By denying the intellect any vision, any apprehension of content (whether intuitive or abstractive), Kant was summing up and expressing with lucid radicalism the most stubborn aspects of modern empiricism, so vitally connected with the deepest tendencies of the modern scientific movement. And by combining with such an empiricist view a sense of the distinctness of the rational as intense as that found in Plato, Kant satisfied both the rationalistic tendencies everlastingly inherent in the scientific spirit and the particular ambitions of modern rationalism. No wonder that the theory of the priority of judgment over concept has been one of the most commonly received features of Kantian influence. Strict empiricism aside, it would probably not be an exaggeration to say that Kantian ideas on the primacy of judgment had been universally received in modern philosophy until Husserl set forth the theory of the *Wesenschau*, and that the only district of modern philosophy (again, strict empiricism aside) not controlled by the Kantian theory of the primacy of judgment is the field influenced by the set purpose of achieving, first of all, a phenomenological description of essences.

Against this doctrinal and historical background, it is easy to set forth the meaning of the issue under consideration. We are suggesting that what was erroneously held by Kantian idealism with regard to theoretical knowledge and to knowledge as a whole does hold in the domain of practical knowledge. Here, without denying the reality of abstraction and without questioning that an intellectual apprehension of intelligible contents exists, without positing any of the postulations of Kant's empiricism or of his rationalism, it must be said that every concept— I mean every formally practical concept—exists in dependence upon some antecedent judgment. The concept of assassination presupposes the judgment that innocent people ought not to be put to death. This is so clear that the use of the word "assassination" would be considered to involve falsehood and defamation if killing was lawful and perhaps obligatory, as it is in self-defense. The concept of theft presupposes the judgments that things can be appropriated and that they ought not to be taken away from their lawful proprietor. The concept of matrimony supposes the judgment that the relations between man and woman cannot be entirely delivered to the control of individual and transient inclinations, but should, to some extent, be regulated by society and contained within the dignity of a social status. The concept of faithfulness presupposes the judgment that it is good to live up to pledges, promises, and contracts. The concept of perjury depends upon the judgment that it is particularly bad to lie under oath. It is unnecessary to multiply examples. The relevant thing is to see that these two propositions, "In moral philosophy, the consideration of human use is essential" and "In moral philosophy—and more generally, in practical thought—judgment is antecedent to concept," convey most closely related meanings. *It is because moral philosophy considers not only natures but also human use that it implies a priority of judgment over concept.* Let us consider, for instance, problems of nature and of use regarding such a tendency as the urge to know. The remark, which Aristotle makes in the opening sentence of the *Metaphysics*,[14] that all men naturally desire to know is a purely theoretical judgment, altogether relative to a fact of nature. We enter into the ethics of the life of knowledge when we begin to wonder what use we should make of the natural urge to know. Should it be considered unimportant, and disquieting by reason of its tendency to divert thought from the world of action? Should it be considered, on the contrary, the loftiest tendency of the rational nature? In the latter theory, encouraging the desire for knowledge will still raise problems of balance, inasmuch as human nature comprises a multiplicity of tendencies and can be damaged, or destroyed, by the disorderly exaltation of any of them, albeit the loftiest. As soon as these problems of use occasion the utterance of distinct concepts—by "distinct" I mean, pertaining with propriety to the understanding of use—we have to do with concepts shaped by the power of judgments about the right and the wrong use of the natural desire for knowledge. In the theory of Aquinas, the concept of studiosity corresponds to the right use of the desire for knowledge and the concept of curiosity to a wrong use of the same desire.[15]

*The Notion of Finality*

An all-important issue remains to be considered. The preceding exposition might suggest that, whereas Kant's judicative formalism is rejected throughout the domain of theoretical knowledge, it is considered to hold in practical matters. Thus we have to tackle this precise question: Is it possible to account for the priority of judgment over the practical concept in a philosophy that asserts the priority of concept over judgment in theoretical knowledge and in knowledge as a whole? The answer to this question is found in the notion of natural finality—a notion systematically repressed in the ethical theory of Kant. Take, for instance, the contrasting concepts of studiosity and curiosity, in which we have recognized marks of essential dependence upon antecedent judgments. Let us consider, in regressive fashion, the genesis of these concepts. Studiosity, indeed, is a concept shaped by the judgment that a certain use of the desire for knowledge is right; the concept of curiosity is no less definitely shaped by the judgment that a certain use of the desire for knowledge is wrong. Now, how were these judgments obtained? By the preceding analysis, these are judgments intrinsically relative to use, intrinsically practical judgments. But these practical judgments were born of judgments about natural finalities, in which the law of the priority of concept over judgment fully obtains, for it is by the understanding of nature, by an exact expression of what a nature is and of what it tends to be, that we are led to judgments of finality. All we have to say, in terms of use, about the excellence of intellectual life derives from theoretical judgments of finality concerning human nature and its powers and functions. Clearly, these judgments of finality are themselves derived from apprehensions of natures, of essences, of whatnesses and of the corresponding tendencies. If the exaltation of studiosity by the moral philosopher is contradicted, say, on the basis of a hedonistic or pragmatic philosophy, the discussion will entirely rest on judgments of finality themselves derived from the understanding of essences and their appropriate expression in concepts. If someone holds, for instance, that the manifest destiny of man is to transform nature rather than to know the laws of the physical, mathematical, and metaphysical worlds, the only relevant argumentation will be based on a comparison between immanent and transitive action and, in the domain of immanent action, on an analysis of the distinctive features of rational knowledge. The concept of studiosity, indeed, presupposes a judgment relative to the use of man's intellectual powers. But this practical judgment, clearly antecedent to the practical concept, is itself derived from a theoretical judgment of finality to which an understanding of essences and tendencies is unqualifiedly anterior. It is the notion of finality which bridges the gap between the study of nature—i.e., the theoretical science—and the study of human use—call it the science of ethics or moral philosophy. In Kant, finality cannot play, as it does in Aristotle and Aquinas, this role of bridge. Besides, the gap is of an entirely different character.

## Truth and Communication

### The Truth of Moral Philosophy

In our discussion of the ultimately practical judgment, we set the notions of theoretical and practical truth in sharp opposition. With reference to this exposition, the problem of the truth that properly pertains to moral philosophy can be stated with clarity. Let us take a typical proposition of moral philosophy, say, "Moral virtues are interdependent" and let us ask whether its truth is theoretical or practical. Obviously, the disjunction is not an exclusive one. Who would question that the precepts of moral philosophy, provided they are genuine, are true by agreement with right desire? How could they be genuine, as moral precepts, if they were, in any way whatsoever, at variance with what right desire demands? The real problem is whether the propositions of moral philosophy are also true theoretically, true in an unqualified sense, true by conformity to a real state of affairs, and whether such is the kind of truth which belongs to them properly and primarily and by reason of their being not prudential but philosophic. The answer cannot be held uncertain. When the moral philosopher asserts, for instance, that moral virtues are interdependent, he means that such is the case, that moral virtues are of such a nature, and are governed by such an essential necessity, that none of them can exist unless all the others are also present. This proposition, considered precisely as an expression of moral philosophy, is true if moral virtues really are interdependent. If they are not, the proposition is unqualifiedly false. When the moral philosopher declares that some actions—say, jealousy—do not admit of any just mean because, even in the slightest amount, they are wrong, he utters a proposition which is true if and only if such actions exist, and which, if no such action exists, is purely and simply false. It can be said that, in the ultimately practical judgment, the failure of a proposition to agree with reality (which failure inevitably occurs in a number of cases by reason of contingency), the theoretical falsehood of a proposition, admits of a redeeming feature, inasmuch as a proposition in disagreement with reality—e.g., I have concluded that such a trip would be good for my family, and a child was killed in a train wreck— may still be true and certain in a practical sense, i.e., by conformity to right desire. It should even be said that such a redeeming feature is redeeming in a decisive sense, inasmuch as practical truth is the only kind of truth that an ultimately practical judgment calls for necessarily and that is due to it. In moral philosophy, a proposition that fails to agree with the real state of affairs is irretrievably false and bad; there is no redeeming feature in it. Either it is true or it is false that some acts are wrong by essence and can never be justified. Either moral virtues are interdependent or they are not. If they are not, the proposition that they are is philosophically false, bad, misleading, obnoxious in every possible respect. The truth of moral philosophy is, primarily and purely and simply, a theoretical truth. It is a relation of conformity between what the intellect asserts or denies and what is really united or separated in the world of things. But, as already suggested, the theoretical truth of moral philosophy, far from excluding its being true by conformity with right desire, strictly demands that it should enjoy such conformity, which is practical truth. Consider, again, the proposition that some actions, like jealousy, admit of no just mean because they are wrong by essence.[16] Such a proposition certainly agrees with right desire, and a man of good character, no matter how ignorant he may be of moral philosophy, will keep away from such actions, and never dream of a moderate dose of jealousy which would be the proper mean between an excess and a defect. Any proposition of moral philosophy that would not agree with right desire would be immoral and false. But, within moral philosophy, this truth by agreement with right desire is a pure consequence of theoretical or unqualified truth. It is not characteristic of moral philosophy; it does not belong to it in strict appropriateness. Insofar as truth by conformity to the real state of affairs is described as the truth of the theoretical intellect, and truth by conformity to right desire as the truth of the practical intellect, moral philosophy is the work of the theoretical intellect.

If we now consider the question of the cause of certitude in the case of moral philosophy as compared with that of the unqualifiedly practical judgment, we shall be led to closely related conclusions. We have seen that in the contingencies of concrete action a judgment never can be certain by reason of antecedent cognition. The antecedent cognitions that we bring forth as we indulge in a vain endeavor to demonstrate that our decision is the right one are always weak in some respect, inasmuch as they involve reference to contingent things, i.e., to things that can be otherwise than they are, in short, to things that are themselves uncertain. And yet a decision born out of a leaky argumentation can enjoy certainty, unqualified assurance, inasmuch as it is ultimately determined by a right inclination toward what is good. Moral philosophy does not admit of leaky argumentations. The certainty of its conclusions proceeds from strict connection with axiomatic premises. Let us be aware that such a law is not brilliantly satisfied in the work of the moral philosophers. No doubt, many of the best conclusions of the best moral philosophers do not enjoy the kind of certainty that a judgment by way of cognition is supposed to possess. This deficient state of affairs can be easily explained by the following reasons. For one thing, in every scientific domain the ratio of conclusions that have reached an entirely scientific state is small: unqualifiedly scientific conclusions are no more than a precious nucleus, the center of organization of the heterogeneous aggregates we call the sciences in our discourses on culture and academic problems. In ethics, failure to achieve the logical rigor without which a conclusion falls short of the scientific condition may be surreptitiously made more likely and frequent by reason of the privileges that judgment by inclination enjoys in moral matters. In other sciences, if a conclusion is not strictly established by way of cognition, the falsehood or the imperfection of the discourse is likely to be noticeable. But in ethics a community of inclination between the writer and the reader may well conceal the fact that a proposition is established only by way of inclination, which is the same as saying that the philosophic work has not yet begun.

*Communicability*

The most striking, if not the most profound, contrast between prudence and moral philosophy involves the communicability of knowledge. Once more, what is really decisive, the final factor of certainty in prudence, is incommunicable. What we communicate when we succeed, as it frequently happens, in convincing our neighbor that our prudential decision was right is a host of inconclusive considerations; these are plausible enough to cause persuasion, as long as there is no particularly strong ground of opposition, but these plausible considerations did not cause the certainty of our conclusion. Its certainty was caused by agreement with right inclination, and this is a cause of certainty that no discourse can communicate. Whoever has had to discharge duties of moral leadership knows that, although much can be done by the sheer power of faith and example, there comes a time when, in order to cause in others adherence to what we know to be right and aversion to what we know to be wrong, we depend on the power of demonstration and communicable knowledge. This is precisely where moral philosophy begins. We might not feel very strongly the need to understand issues that are already settled by the unchecked power of our love and our hatred; in other words, we might not feel that it is important to utter judgments by way of cognition about issues already settled by judgments by way of inclination if we did not experience the need for a communication guaranteed by the rational necessity of demonstrative knowledge. It seems that such a need is not experienced at all times, in all societies, and under all circumstances. When the thing we are concerned with is not so much the communication of knowledge as unanimous adherence to a rule of action, the weight of tradition, the magic of conformity, the prestige of common memories, the appeal of heroic personalities—whether genuine or mythical—and more subtle ways by which group affections shape the affections and the judgments of the individuals suffice to bring about the needed unity. No doubt it should even be said that any method of rational communication which jeopardizes these forces of unanimity is a threat to the unity of community feeling and community action. This is what the judges of Socrates seem to have understood very well. With regard to unity in judging about the right and the wrong, the history of societies is divided into a pre-Socratic and a Socratic age. We do not mean only that an important novelty took place in the history of the world when Socrates contributed decisively to the foundation of moral philosophy. We also mean that it can happen at any time in the history of a particular community that an issue on which sufficient agreement (an amount of agreement having about the same effects as consensus) had, so far, been ensured by affective communion no longer can be satisfactorily treated by such spontaneous methods, and demands to be treated by methods of rational communication. With regard to this particular issue, this particular society is in transition from the pre-Socratic to the Socratic age. Such transitions always have the character of crises, and they inevitably involve considerable destructions. One may not even be entitled to hope that the amount of agreement to be obtained in the future by methods of rational communication will ever equal the amount of agreement that was obtained in the past, spontaneously and silently, by affective communion. This is why the judges of Socrates always remain, in all societies, wakeful and suspicious. At all times, but particularly in phases of swift development, the most characteristic of which is the age of modern science and technology, they have very good reasons to contend that the new ways never will give society the same unity and stability as the old ones. Their reasons are so good that at all times these gentlemen deserve to be treated with some respect. And yet the transition from the pre-Socratic to the Socratic age, with regard to an ever-growing number of issues, belongs to the logic of history. By this expression, so often used in detestable ambiguity, we intend to designate all the processes that, *by reason of what human nature is*, should occur *normally* as men take advantage of the work of preceding generations. The development of sciences and techniques belongs to the logic of history; this does not mean that it ever had the inevitability of a physical process, and this does not rule out the possibility of a new scientific and technical Dark Ages that would be brought about by gigantic destructions. All it means is that the relation of human nature to knowledge being what it is, the transition from Ptolemy to Galileo and to Newton to Einstein was well in line with the idea, the logos, immanent in human nature. The celebrated passage in which Pascal likens the scientific development of mankind to the processes of learning in an individual man expresses one aspect—indeed, the best-known and perhaps the least mysterious aspect—of the logic of history. Likewise, it is normal that the truth about human affairs be gradually discovered through the work of generations. But let it be pointed out that this normal progress in moral knowledge involves two widely different aspects: it involves, on the one hand, transition from ignorance or error to the cognition of what is true, and, on the other, *within the knowledge of the true*, transition from judgment by way of mere inclination to judgment by way of cognition. The contrast between the pre-Socratic and the Socratic age concerns the latter transition rather than the former. There was a time, in a not very remote past, when it was commonly held that in a just war the extermination of prisoners was a matter of course, an action just by the very justice of the war. We have come to understand that when an individual recently engaged in an unjust collective action has been forced away from this injustice, he has recovered a right to an entire presumption of innocence and ought to be treated as an entirely innocent person as long as he consents to stay away from the unjust action of his fellow countrymen, in other words, as long as he consents to remain a non-belligerent. In a case such as this, the transition is from ignorance and error to the knowledge of the true. Let us now consider cases in which there is transition—or need for a transition—from true judgment by way of mere inclination to true judgment not only by inclination but also by cognition and rational understanding. It is all too easy to find examples in the moral crisis of modern times. The most obvious of these examples concerns the respect for human life and the ethics of matrimony. Although all moral errors, no matter how monstrous, have always been lavishly represented both in the actions and in the thoughts of men, it is possible to point to periods—to avoid arbitrariness and empty talk we would have to be very particular about the subjects, the societies, and the periods under consideration—when some sort of consensus, sufficient for many social purposes, existed by way of affective communion about such subjects as the evil of infanticide (unborn infants not excluded), the evil of murdering incurably sick people, the preferability of matrimony to free union, the prohibition of incest and homosexuality, etc. Since the nineteenth century it has become necessary, and it will remain necessary forever, to explain to an ever-growing number of people why those things are wrong. The working out of these explanations may be tragically difficult. But we know that we have no choice. The times of exclusive dependence upon judgment by inclination are gone forever. This realization of an historic need does not imply any underestimation of the value and the irreplaceable power of knowledge by inclination. But it seems that the very preservation of knowledge by inclination demands that something be done along the line of explanation. Again, the risk is tragic: it is a great disaster to replace a virtuous instinct by a mere rudiment of science. Yet no matter how great the risk, we often feel that we have no choice, that the urge toward understanding is rendered irresistible by the forces of history, and that some sort of progress toward explanation has become necessary for the preservation of whatever is left of virtuous instinct and correct judgment by inclination. With no illusion about the possibility of bringing about demonstrative knowledge in a great number of minds, we trust that some good can be done, provided the direction followed by our very imperfectly demonstrative argumentations is sound, provided it is the right direction, the one that will certainly lead some day to demonstrative knowledge, even though in a small number of minds.

Much can be learned about practical knowledge and moral philosophy by considering the nature of this urge, so abundantly manifested by the history of moral ideas in modern times, toward the explanation of moral issues, and the general sentiment that judgment about moral affairs by mere inclination has lost its self-sufficiency. What is it that carries all parts of moral thought into a Socratic age obviously crowded with dangers? A shallow answer would put the blame upon the viciousness of rationalistic philosophers. We may obtain a more profound one by considering again the relation between the fulfillment and the explanation of moral rules. (This may even render the success of rationalistic philosophies intelligible.) So far, we have seen that the ultimately practical judgment is primarily concerned with fulfillment, and that the work of the moral philosopher is primarily concerned with explanation. The time has come to ask whether there would not be, beyond this significant contrast, an illuminating aspect of unity between fulfillment and explanation.

In this reconsideration, we first need to exemplify the separation of fulfillment and explanation. To admit of exact fulfillment, the command given by a superior, assuming that it lies within the actual power of the inferior, need only be unambiguous; its reasons may remain entirely undisclosed. If, for instance, a subordinate officer, in war or in war games, is ordered to move his troops a certain distance and in a certain direction, all that is needed for the order to admit of complete fulfillment is that it state unequivocally the direction of the movement and the distance to be covered, and decide such questions as whether the movement must be effected at any cost or given up in case of strong resistance. We say that an order is clear when it rules out ambiguity on all such issues. This clarity concerns purely a matter of fact; it is relative to the fact *that* there is such and such an order, not to the reasons *why* it is such and such. What does the general staff expect of this movement? What part does this movement play in what strategy? Absolute secrecy on these subjects may not impair or endanger the fulfillment of the order. Here, we have a clear case of fulfillment without explanation.

There is no need to elaborate on the corresponding possibility of explanation without fulfillment: moral philosophers are commonly suspected of not fulfilling the rules that they explain so well.

Instead of a manmade command, such as an order given by the general staff to a subordinate officer, let us now consider fulfillment and explanation in relation to a rule of natural morality. In business transactions it is not always easy to see what is fair and what is not; this is a field in which dependable moralists are divided not only with regard to prudential issues, intrinsically modified by historical contingencies, but even with regard to definite entities. Let us consider, for instance, the question whether it is always lawful for a seller to seek all the profit that the unsophisticated market allows. (By saying "unsophisticated market" we mean to leave out of the picture such fraudulent situations as can be brought about, say, by the spreading of false news.) Stories from the good old days speak of shopkeepers who voluntarily kept prices below what the purchaser was willing to pay, just because they held that a bigger profit would have been unreasonable; they looked with suspicion at quickly made fortunes. To be sure, such sense of honesty has not disappeared from the world. Why do we place these stories in the past? Perhaps out of a frustrated mood inspired by the hardships of the present. Whether the ratio of honest business people has increased or diminished, recent generations have witnessed a growing demand for social institutions and legal dispositions tending to exclude arbitrariness and fortuitousness from the judgment that a determinate value is balanced by another determinate value. Socialism, the labor and co-operative movements, predominating trends in taxation policies, and the institutionalism of free distribution—all these trends so noticeable in the evolution of modern societies convey, among largely heterogeneous meanings, the view that justice in exchanges requires more than the unsophisticated condition of the market. Beyond certain limits the chance occurrences of the market threaten to disrupt the balance of the values exchanged by making it possible to build a fortune through little service or to purchase much service with little money. It can be doubted that the work of the moralists on these obscure subjects has actually resulted in conclusions demonstratively connected with the first principles of the science of justice. An entire trend in the development of public conscience points to the expression of a law that we are hardly able to formulate, much less to explain with intelligible rigor.

## NOTES

1. The "purpose" or "end" of a science belongs to it intrinsically. A theoretical science can be used for practical purposes, as in the case

of the engineer who studies geometry without the slightest interest in scientific explanation. What is practical here is the scientist; the science remains altogether theoretical. Let this be entirely clear: whenever we describe a science as theoretical or practical by reason of its purpose, we refer to a purpose of such character as to modify the epistemological structure of the science under consideration. When a theoretical science is used for practical purposes, it does not become practical, except with regard to an accidental condition of no relevance from an epistemological standpoint. This point is developed more fully below, pp. 51–52.

2. 96Aff.

3. Friedrich Nietzsche, *The Birth of Tragedy*, trans. Francis Golffing (Garden City, N.Y.: Doubleday, 1956), p. 51.

4. *The City of God* VIII, 3.

5. "Socrates, the Founder of Moral Science," *Historical Studies in Philosophy*, trans. Fred Rothwell (London: Macmillan, 1912), pp. 8–73.

6. *Metaphysics* I, 6, 987B1.

7. Ibid. XIII, 4, 1078B30.

8. *Nicomachean Ethics* I, 3, 1095A4.

9. This word was coined by Jacques Maritain (see in particular his *The Degrees of Knowledge*, trans. Gerald B. Phelan [New York: Scribner's, 1959]). In our opinion it should displace all the adjectives used to designate the non-philosophical approach to nature. "Experimental" is too narrow, since it refers to a method characterized by the predominant use of experiments, i.e., of processes caused according to human plans for the purpose of observation; "positive" inevitably connotes the notion of science which characterizes positivism; "empirical science" is an intolerable contradiction inasmuch as "scientific" is said in direct opposition to "empirical." But in "empiriological" we have both the broadest reference to experience and all the demands that follow upon the assertion of rationality. "Empiriological" speaks of an experience organized by an intelligible principle. It refers not to sheer experience, but to experience with a soul of intelligibility, ἐμπειρία μετὰ λόγου.

10. For amplification of this point, see the letter of Yves Simon to Jacques Maritain, dated February 15, 1961, included in the appendix to chap. 3, pp. 106–107.

11. Augustine, *On Free Choice* II, 19; Thomas Aquinas, *Summa theol.* I–II, 55, 4.

12. Thomas Aquinas, *Summa theol.* I–II, 8–17.

13. Etienne Gilson, "Pourquoi saint Thomas a critiqué saint Augus-

tin," *Archives d'Histoire Doctrinale et Littéraire du Moyen Age*, 1 (1926), 5–127.

14. 980A22.

15. *Summa theol.* II–II, 166–67.

16. It is hardly necessary to recall that propositions of this type demand a very exacting ascertainment of the terms involved. "Jealousy" here does not designate a mere emotion which might be involuntary, inevitable, or even perfectly normal, but voluntary indulgence in sadness about what is genuinely good for another person.

# 3

# Disputed Questions

## The Problem of Practically Practical Science

MORAL PHILOSOPHY IS FITTINGLY DESCRIBED as a theoretically practical science. Let us discuss some of its relations with other ways of practical knowledge. One aspect of this question has been treated briefly in Chapter 1. If practical wisdom is considered on the level of total practicality, its concern is fulfillment rather than explanation. However, the fulfillment of the laws of a rational being ought to be rational. Insofar as moral philosophy contributes to the understanding of what we have to do, it is connected with a demand pertaining to prudence and ultimate practicality. We should emphasize that the extreme of practicality contains a demand for the extreme of intelligibility.

In Chapter 2 we remarked that the distance between moral philosophy and prudence is often great. This is an experience familiar to moral philosophers; when they have said their last word, they are still immensely far from knowing what we have to do under the circumstances that are ours. People resent this and cannot understand why philosophers, after having formulated and vindicated principles, are unable, or unwilling, to give them the slightest information about what could be done to apply these principles. Correspondingly, many philosophers—to say nothing of theologians, whose predicament, in this respect, is not any better—go beyond what the philosophical method allows, and deliver in print a lump made of philosophy and of something else that is closer to the problems of action. This procedure is acceptable only if the epistemological situation is clear, and if the philosopher does not try to make the reader believe that his more concrete conclusions were attained by philosophic ways. In many cases they are attained by way of inclination, and are not more dependable than the inclinations of the person who happens to be a moral philosopher.

Whoever has realized the distance between the level of moral philosophy and that of prudence can hardly help asking the following question: Does there exist, somewhere between moral philosophy and prudence, any distinct epistemological entity, less abstract and less explanatory but more practical than philosophy, less practical but more general, and closer to the scientific ideal, than prudence? Is there such a thing as practically practical science?

This question has been discussed with much thoroughness by Jacques Maritain in several papers, the most fundamental of which is the chapter in *The Degrees of Knowledge* entitled "St. John of the Cross, Practitioner of Contemplation."[1] Our purpose does not go beyond giving a correct exposition of Maritain's ideas on this subject, with an effort to show what the main difficulties are and what lines of inquiry should be followed in the further treatment of these difficulties.

The point of departure of Maritain's research is the seeming divergence between two religious writers, St. Thomas Aquinas and St. John of the Cross. As far as externals and the letter of statements are concerned, the two saints seem to disagree sharply on some important issues. For instance, whereas St. Thomas describes contemplation as the highest kind of activity, St. John of the Cross describes it as a state of non-acting. And yet the reader familiar with them both has a feeling that they do not disagree and that the contrast between their expressions is accounted for by epistemological differences, i.e., differences pertaining to their ways of knowing, to their standpoints, to the kinds of knowledge that they are exercising, not to their judgments on issues phrased in one and the same way.

Trouble may be caused by the fact that the point of departure of Maritain's research is theological. No matter what we have to say about the discrepancies between the epistemological ways of St. Thomas and those of St. John of the Cross, these discrepancies cannot amount to the distinction of two sciences. Theology is one science. The distinction of the theoretical and the practical does not disrupt its unity, much less a distinction that is supposed to take place within the practical part of theological consideration. Thus, if we are going to define two distinct ways of knowledge, let us never forget that, in the case that is the point of departure for Maritain's research, this distinction between ways of knowledge cannot amount to the distinction of two sciences.

Maritain soon remarks that the epistemological treatment of such a subject as contemplation by St. Thomas is akin to a philosophic treatment, whereas the treatment found in St. John of the Cross resembles the kind of approach characteristic of those thinkers whom we call moralists (such as Montaigne or Irving Babbitt) but not moral philosophers (such as Aristotle).

The characteristics of moral philosophy, according to Maritain, are those we expounded in Chapter 2. For him, moral philosophy is a *theoretically practical science*. This expression occurs again and again in his writings. It is, in his mind, of decisive importance, inasmuch as the adverb of manner "theoretically" conveys the theoretical character of whatever pertains to the *mode*, the method, the way, of defining and dividing that characterize moral philosophy. The ways of the moralist, on the contrary, his method, the way in which he shapes his concepts, defines, and divides, are essentially affected by the practical character of his concern. For Maritain the science of the moralist is a *practically practical science*.

Let us try to define its practicality as located between that of prudence, on the one hand, and that of moral philosophy, on the other. As we saw in the first chapter, in prudence, the synthetic method is characterized by a *totality of consideration* equal to the complexity of the case. True, prudence may answer general questions; in fact, it often does substitute for moral philosophy in dealing with issues that a moral philosopher is not ready to treat. It also happens that the answer of prudence is more likely to be understood and accepted than the answer of philosophy. This is an interesting paradox, since *de jure* philosophy is communicable and explanatory, whereas prudence is neither. But the advantage as well as the characteristic of prudence is the ability to carry out a synthesis equal to the complexity of the relevant factors of individual and perhaps strictly unique cases.

At the opposite end of the line, the synthetic character of

moral philosophy consists merely in its essential consideration of use. There is practical synthesis in moral philosophy only insofar as such synthesis follows upon the consideration of use.

Between the two, the practically practical science of Maritain is a science of practical mode. Not only is it concerned with right and wrong use, but it is practical, and synthetic in the way characteristic of practical knowledge, in its approach to things, i.e., in its way of understanding things and of expressing them in concepts and definitions. Maritain insists on this, and at this point obviously sees the crux of the matter: whereas the concepts of moral philosophy express, with no further ado, the result of an abstraction, i.e., of an operation intended to make an intelligible structure accessible to the intellect, the concepts of practically practical science already bear the mark of the practical method. In moral philosophy the practical job, whatever it may be, is done with concepts whose law of constitution is, just as it would be in a purely theoretical science, a determination to express that which is. In terminology that is ours, not Maritain's, the concepts of moral philosophy answer the theoretical question "What are the things?" just as if we were in a purely theoretical science. On the other hand, the concepts of practically practical science are engaged in an answer to a practical question. Recall that the practical question *par excellence* is the question "What ought we to do?" Let us give an example. When St. Thomas says that contemplation is the highest kind of activity, he uses the concept of contemplation—which is designed to say that the thing called contemplation is—in answer to the theoretical question "What is the thing?" St. Thomas' concept of contemplation says that it is an act rather than a state of potency, a second act rather than a first act, an immanent act rather than a transitive one, a terminal act rather than an intermediary one, and, among the actions that are immanent and ultimate, the loftiest in nature. The question answered by St. John of the Cross's concept, on the contrary, answers (perhaps it should be said "in part") practical questions of the following type: In order to be contemplating, what ought we to do? What are we going to do? In this way contemplation, envisaged from a practical standpoint, appears as a state of non-acting.

Maritain concentrates on the problem of conceptualization. At the same level of inquiry one might raise the problem of explanation. Much can be learned by comparing the ways of conceptualization with those of explanation. The fundamental consideration here is that a concept is in a way an answer to a question. The mode of conceptualization is determined by the kind of question that we propose to answer. This is crucial: in the treatment of the epistemological mode, conceptualization would not be ultimate. Ultimacy would belong to explanation. This agrees nicely with those sections of elementary logic which compare the three operations of the mind with one another, and perfection in validity with the logical perfection which comprises, besides valid inference, the final qualities of truth, certainty, and explanation. Is there such a thing as a practical explanation? The expression may be uncommon, but the thing seems to be the most common in the world. In daily life as well as in historical research, we constantly ask for the explanation of things that do not admit of any theoretical explanation. These things are engaged in contingency, and involve a plurality of causes that is not unified by any essence; accordingly, if there were to be a theoretical explanation, the explanatory process would go on indefinitely, and branch indefinitely many times. Meyerson, at the beginning of *Identity and Reality*,[2] uses the following example: I missed my train today because my watch was late. It is the fault of the Greeks because if the Greeks had been defeated by the Persians, there would probably be no watches and no trains. My answer is absurd and arbitrary because my question was practical. The real meaning of the question "Why did I miss my train?" was "What am I going to do in order not to miss my train again?" The accident of my missing the train is explained inasmuch as the practical question borne in mind is answered. The same accident admits of no theoretical explanation: I would have to go farther back than the Greeks and the Persians and do the same along indefinitely many branching lines. In order not to miss my train again, I will make sure that my watch has the correct time. Suppose an answer of a widely different type, such as "I missed my train today because traffic in the city was slowed down by thick fog; the taxicab that took me to the train station made the trip in twenty minutes instead of five." Here again I am answering a practical question. To the question "What shall I do in order not to miss my train again?" I answer that, at some times of the year at least, it is a good precaution to check the fog situation early enough to be able, if necessary, to procure a cab half an hour earlier than usual. The explanation of the notion of practical explanation should be carried out as far as possible along the line of the analogy between theoretical and practical cognition. We might be tempted to say that explanation is an essentially theoretical process, so that there is no such thing as a practical explanation. The analysis of examples such as Meyerson's serves to show that there is indeed such a thing as a practical explanation. If there is a paradox in the concept of practical explanation, it is no greater than the paradox in the concept of truth, and that is one, not of cognition, but of direction. Practical explanation is related to theoretical explanation as practical truth is related to theoretical truth. These two ratios are not the only ones that can be declared similar in a system of proportionality designed to explain the concept of practical explanation. But the ratio $\frac{\text{practical truth}}{\text{theoretical truth}}$ is apparently the last one and the best in terms of strict appropriateness. Before the ratio between the two truths I would place the ratio between the cognitions, theoretical and practical. We thus have at least these three:

$$\frac{\text{Practical explanation}}{\text{Theoretical explanation}} = \frac{\text{Practical knowledge}}{\text{Theoretical knowledge}} = \frac{\text{Practical truth}}{\text{Theoretical truth}}.$$

In practical explanation, we are not aware of carrying out such an absurd explanation when, considering, for instance, an historical failure, we ask the question "Why did he fail?" and feel satisfied with an answer obtained after a finite number of steps. We did not stop the inquiry arbitrarily, or just out of fatigue. We actually got the answer; it was an answer to a practical question. The real question was: "Suppose that we want to do what he failed to achieve, *what should we do* in order not to fail as he did? Or suppose we want any similar attempt to be doomed to failure, again what should we do?" It seems that in the theory of practically practical science such views on practical explanation should normally accompany Maritain's views on practical conceptualization.[3]

Attention should be called to a difficulty which, so far as I know, has not been extensively treated in the work of Jacques Maritain. If a discipline is such that its law of conceptualization is practical; if it is such that its concepts answer practical questions; with greater force, if a discipline is such that its law of explanation is practical, is it still a science? The notion of science upheld in the *Posterior Analytics* is defined by the union of certainty and explanation. A science is a discipline whose explanations are certain and whose certainties are explanatory. We hold that history is not a science. Yet it often deals with facts that are established with certainty, and it often gives answers to the question "Why?" But its explanations, if considered theoretically, are uncertain. The explanatory process, by reason of contingency, would go on indefinitely, and branch indefinitely many times, as we saw in Meyerson's example. We stop it without arbitrariness when we have obtained a practical explanation in answer to a practical question that, most of the time, remains unformulated.

My suggestion is that in the so-called practically practical sciences a practical conceptualization is determined by something more profound and more decisive, viz., the asking of practical questions. The explanation that the practically practical discipline supplies, through the operation of concepts that have been constructed according to a practical law, is a practical explanation. Again, a science is a discipline whose certainties are explanatory and whose explanations are certain. We wonder whether the explanations that enter into the definition of science are necessarily theoretical explanations, explanations of the analytical type. Can there be a science whose *certain* explanations are of the practical type? An answer in the negative seems by far the more probable. Notice that such an answer is the only one compatible with Aristotle's division of the intellectual habitus. If the explanations supplied by a scientific discipline can afford to be purely practical, then it is not right to say that science *is* a theoretical habitus. At most we would be allowed to say that science and explanation are theoretical by priority and practical by posteriority.

Very close to this difficulty is another one involving the origin and character of *certainty* in practically practical disciplines. We should not forget that in the definition of science certainty refers, not to the perfect establishment of any kind of truth, but definitely to the firmness of explanation. Thus, if practically practical sciences exist, their explanations, which are practical explanations, must be certain. Let us inquire into the origin and causes of their certainty. It seems that the origin and the cause of certainty is necessarily either analysis into self-evident truth or the indefectible rightness of virtue. In the first case, we have a certainty of scientific description; in the second case, certainty is prudential, not scientific.

Our conclusion is that *a discipline describable as practically practical cannot be a science*, even if due allowance is made for the analogical amplitude of this term. For one thing, the explanation that science implies is one of theoretical character. For another, there is no source of certitude which would belong in distinct fashion to practically practical disciplines. Either the source of certainty in explanation is an analysis into first premises, and then the scientific *mode* is theoretical; or the origin of certainty in explanation lies in the rightness of virtue, and then we are dealing, not with any kind of science, but with some sort of prudence.

At the beginning of this discussion we called attention to the theological point of departure of Maritain's inquiry. This theological point of departure—which remains the center throughout the discussion—causes a *particular* situation, which would not obtain in purely rational cases. No matter how strong the distinction between the theoretically practical and the practically practical, it cannot disrupt the unity of the theological habitus. Once more, nothing can disrupt it, not even the deeper distinction between the theoretical and the practical. Because of this unity of the theological habitus, the practically practical knowledge, of which Maritain finds the best examples in St. John of the Cross, remains for him a work of science.[4] Because of the unity of the theological habitus, a discipline that is practical in mode, a practically practical discipline, retains something scientific about it. It is a special development of a scientific habitus. In our opinion, the accident of this theological focus is what causes Maritain to attribute a scientific character to practically practical knowledge. Where the factors causing the superior unity of theology are not at work, there exist indeed practically practical disciplines, but they are not scientific. Consider again examples of men who properly speaking are "moralists—not philosophers but practitioners of the science of morals" such as Montaigne, Pascal, Nietzsche, Shakespeare, Racine, Baudelaire, Swift, Meredith, Balzac, and Dostoevski.[5] Some of these are literary creators to whom it never occurred that there was anything scientific about their acquaintance with the human heart. Even in Montaigne and Pascal you find no eagerness to take on the systematic forms that are natural to every science. It is not by accident that the knowledge of the moralists avoided systematic forms. By giving his great work the title of *Essays* Montaigne warns us of his desire to remain conversational and unsystematic in his expositions. Had Pascal not died so prematurely, his great work would not have remained in the state of disconnected or loosely connected "fragments." But we have every reason to believe that its organization would have been that of a book of apologetics, and this is another story.

Practically practical disciplines do exist. The expression "practically practical knowledge" characterizes well the kind of knowledge that we find in this extremely important work of human thought, the work of the moralists. It is valuable and, again, extremely important without being scientific. In a state of achievement that it rarely attains, it is found somewhere between moral philosophy and prudence.[6]

## Ethics and Christian Philosophy

Let us recall the great discussions that went on, in the late '20s and early '30s, on the subject of "Christian Philosophy."[7] To understand the meaning of these discussions, it is good to bear in mind that not so many years before there had been—to a considerable extent in the same circles—very ardent discussions on the general relations between philosophical knowledge and faith. In this earlier period, the great question was whether philosophy was a pure work of reason or a product of a commitment of "the whole soul." For those who upheld the theory of philosophy as work of the whole soul, with strong emphasis on the significant role played, in the life and in the understanding of the philosopher, by the *heart*, the *will*, love of truth, readiness to believe, etc., there could hardly be any question of a philosophic knowledge free from intrinsic dependence on faith. The great concern was to ensure the vital cooperation of faith and of whatever was called philosophic knowledge. Did the representatives of this trend maintain that faith propositions play an *intrinsic* role in philosophical research? Clear statements on such issues were generally avoided, but the prevailing tendency favored the confusion of faith and philosophical knowledge. The Thomists were ardently disliked in circles where these tendencies prevailed, for any Thomist is pledged to maintain that philosophy is a work of reason, a thing entirely natural, whose principles are entirely contained in natural experience and in the natural perception of self-evident premises. A Thomist may consider it desirable that philosophy and faith not be separated in the mind of the believer who happens to be a philosopher. But he would emphasize the difference between separating and distinguishing. No matter how desirable it may be that philosophy and faith not be separated, a Thomist would insist that they ought to be, and to remain under all circumstances, distinct.

The discussions of the late '20s and early '30s on the subject of Christian philosophy were conducted, not exclusively but to a large extent, by philosophers known for their adherence to the doctrines of St. Thomas Aquinas. The whole sequence of those discussions started with an exposition by Etienne Gilson whose point of view was principally that of an historian of ideas. For Gilson Christian philosophy was, first of all, an historical reality, the historical reality of philosophical thoughts that, over a long period of time and under a great diversity of circumstances, existed undeveloped in close association with, and under the influence of, Christian faith. Another historian of philosophy, Emile Bréhier, not a Thomist indeed, held that Christian philosophy had no more reality than Christian mathematics or Christian physics. Father Mandonnet, who did so much over his long career for the exact knowledge of St. Thomas' work, and who certainly deserved to be considered a Thomist, was not far from upholding the paradox of Emile Bréhier. For him the immensity of the distance between the rational truths that make up philosophy and the revealed propositions that express mysteries—that is, truth that is not naturally accessible to any created or creatable intellect, but only to God Himself—ruled out the union of the two knowledges, knowledge by faith and philosophical knowledge, in any whole that could be relevantly called a Christian philosophy.

As could be expected, much confusion clouded these discussions. Maritain's book *On Christian Philosophy* provided some desirable clarification. In this work, Maritain distinguishes between the *nature* of philosophy and its state. As far as nature is concerned, philosophy is made of natural and rational knowledge, and that is all we have to say. But, by reason of its subject, this body of natural and rational knowledge admits of a variety of states. It would be nonsensical to speak of a Christian state of mathematics or physics. But philosophy is concerned, in its own way, with God and with human destiny, and because it deals with these subjects, it admits of a Christian state. Is it in an intrinsic sense that we speak of Christian philosophy? In my opinion a consideration is not intrinsic unless it pertains to the nature that is being studied. Determinations pertaining not to nature but to state remain extrinsic, but extrinsic does not mean unimportant. It is extrinsically that a system of philosophy is described as Christian. But the Christian state, in which a number of philosophic systems have developed, may be of great relevance for the understanding of philosophical history and for the understanding of the conditions in which the philosophic sciences develop best in the human mind.

In *On Christian Philosophy*, Maritain made the important and often ignored point that, as far as its relation to faith is concerned, the case of practical philosophy is distinct from that of theoretical philosophy. Briefly, theoretical philosophy, like all theoretical sciences, is concerned with understanding what the things are in the necessity of their universal essences. This necessity is absolute; it is one with the necessity of the principle of identity, and cannot be altered by existential differences. On the contrary, practical knowledge, even on the high level of abstraction which is that of philosophy, is concerned with what we have to do. Accordingly, considerations pertaining to existence and state are relevant. The least that can be said is that it cannot be taken for granted that in the state of his Christian destiny man has to do exactly the same as what he would have had to do in the state of a purely natural destiny. There is a reluctance on the part of many to perceive the basic difference between theoretical and practical philosophy when the relation to faith and revelation is involved. The strongest reason for this reluctance seems to be the fear that fundamentals concerning natural law and natural virtue may be endangered and that some sort of fideism may invade practical philosophy.

Let us discuss the various kinds of discrepancy which may be conceived between a purely natural ethics and the ethics that holds unconditionally for the Christian in the Christian state of existence:

(1) Revelation determines new duties, unknown to natural ethics, and whose notion makes no sense in terms of natural ethics, e.g., the duty to receive the sacraments. This is not what causes difficulty. As long as the novelty resulting from the Christian state in which we live is purely added to the precepts of natural ethics, there is no epistemological problem.

(2) The epistemological problem begins when a statement that would hold unconditionally in a purely natural state of affairs is in some way at variance with a corresponding statement modified by considerations relative to the Christian state in which we exist. Included here are all propositions answering questions precisely relative, not to our nature, but to the state in which we exist. Obviously the very first question of all ethics, viz., the question of the last end, is one of them. A purely rational answer would say what the last end of man would be in the state natural to man. But in order to avoid all misunderstanding, this answer should be accompanied by something like the following remark: the last end of man would not be precisely what we said if man existed in a state different from the state that is natural to him. What the factual situation is, philosophy does not know. And so, concerning the first and the most decisive problem of ethics, we obtain only a conditional answer: an answer that leaves aside the matter of *fact*. Now, practical knowledge—I mean any knowledge that is practical in a proper sense, even though it may

remain theoretical in important respects—is intrinsically and essentially concerned with matters of fact, because it is essentially concerned with the direction of human action. Even if knowledge remains at a great distance from the level of action, as is the case in moral philosophy, its answers must hold in terms of facts or of factual situations. Otherwise it would not say the truth about the right and the wrong use of our freedom and could not aim at directing human action. To the question "What is the last end of man?" any science that is practical in a proper sense, that is concerned with the right and the wrong in the use of our freedom, and proposes to direct human action, must be able to give a true answer. Now, true answers to such questions cannot be had except by revelation.

(3) Closely related to this is the following issue: the change in the last end which is brought about by the fact of man's supernatural destiny entails corresponding changes in the general conditions of right life. Moral virtues retain their names; they still are called prudence, justice, fortitude, and temperance as they were in Aristotle, in Plato, and in the Pythagoreans. Definitions are unaltered—indeed, definitions refer to natures and essences, not to states. But when we ask what conditions the steady practice of, say, courageous action must satisfy in order to be the virtue of fortitude, with all the implications of the notion of virtue as distinct from lower-ranking forms of excellence, then it is necessary to turn to the novelties brought into human destiny by the fact of a supernatural last end. By reason of what the last end of man is in man's factual destiny, fortitude will not be a virtue unless it is animated by charity. Among considerations of this kind, a particularly significant one relates to the connection, or interdependence, of moral virtues. If everything in man's destiny were natural, we would say that virtues are interdependent for two reasons. (*a*) Every particular virtue requires *modes* supplied by other virtues. In order to be temperate or just, it is often necessary to display a great deal of fortitude. It is necessary to be temperate with fortitude. (*b*) Moral virtues are connected in prudence. It would be pleasant to fancy that in order to judge truthfully in matters of justice, the only virtue presupposed is justice itself. But even if it were possible (contrary to the views just set forth) to possess justice

without possessing fortitude and temperance, these virtues would be needed for our judgments to be prudent in matters of justice as well as in any matter. To be sure, a man cannot be said to possess prudent judgment in matters of justice if the rightness of his judgment in these matters is habitually threatened by desires that temperance does not control or by weaknesses and cowardice that no fortitude overcomes. Thus we have two grounds for the interdependence of moral virtues. The statement "these grounds are two" is supposed to be absolutely true, without any particular postulate or hypothesis. But when we think of the last end of man in his supernatural destiny, a third ground appears, which is charity. In the Christian state of human existence, the grounds of the interdependence of virtues are not two but three. That they are three cannot be known except by revelation. The old answer in terms of two grounds has become false inasmuch as it has become incomplete. Now when the moral philosopher is asked about the grounds of the interdependence of moral virtues, he cannot be allowed to answer that the grounds are two when they actually are three. His answer would not only be incomplete; it would also be false. Again, a discipline concerned with the right and the wrong in the use of human freedom and with the direction of human action is necessarily concerned with matters of fact. (c) Lastly comes a question which worries many: Can there conceivably be cases in which what is declared right by the purely natural and rational knowledge of ethics would be declared wrong by an ethical position aware of what the supernatural destiny of man implies?

In the discussion of this issue let us bear in mind that there is a fundamental difference between the cases in which the mean of virtue is determined by a thing (*medium rei*) and the cases in which it is determined by an act of the reason (*medium rationis*). The situation of justice is unique, for the mean of this virtue is determined by a thing; accordingly, *it is independent of changes in our existential condition.* If I have received a loan of a hundred dollars, with no interest, the sum that I am supposed to return is exactly one hundred dollars regardless of whether the human condition is purely natural or not, and regardless of whether the last end of man is natural or supernatural. The issue is settled by a thing, and that thing is one hundred dollars, neither more nor less, under all circumstances.

The case is different when the mean is determined by an act of the reason. Then a change in the last end *may* cause a change in the proper mean, for it is in relation to a determinate end that an action possesses the character of a proper mean. A famous example concerns temperance. The extreme forms of asceticism practiced by many great saints puzzle most moral philosophers and arouse the indignation of many. Natural ethics and Christian ethics recommend temperance. They would agree that particularly difficult acts of temperance, implying more than what is needed for good health and lucid understanding, are commendable, once in a while, inasmuch as they guarantee self-control and independence from passions which always convey a threat of disorder. But it is perfectly intelligible that natural ethics and Christian ethics may be at variance with regard to the extreme forms of asceticism. Here one says yes and the other says no. The extreme forms of asceticism are not justifiable in natural ethics, except insofar as natural ethics cannot positively exclude the possibility of changes resulting from a supernatural destiny. Should it be said that on such a subject as the extreme forms of asceticism natural ethics and Christian ethics contradict each other? Indeed, extreme forms of asceticism are considered lawful and necessary by Christian ethics in cases that may be rare. They are held immoral by natural ethics. There is nothing puzzling about such a contradiction, which originates in a more fundamental contradiction concerning the last end of man. Here also, and first of all, natural reason says that the case is such and such, and faith declares that the case is different. Let us be fully aware of such a significant opposition. At the same time, let us never lose sight of the indirect way which safeguards unity. To the question of whether extreme forms of asceticism are lawful and commendable, the answer of the moral philosopher, if it were completely unfolded, would be something like this: these extreme forms of asceticism are neither commendable nor lawful unless the last end of man is changed by a supernatural calling of which, *qua* philosopher, *qua* bearer of a purely rational habitus, the moral philosopher is not aware. The answer of the moral philosopher becomes entirely true by taking on a character of *conditionality* which is thoroughly uncongenial to practical thought, as a result of practical thought's intrinsic concern for the right and the wrong in human use and for the direction of human action.

It was easy to find in the order of temperance ways of acting that are acknowledged by Christian wisdom though not by natural ethics. It would be similarly easy to find examples in the moral virtue of fortitude. As to prudence, its case is the clearest since this virtue has as its purpose finding the right means to ends that may be changed by a change in our existential condition. Again, the case of justice is different and unique because of the settlement of issues by the *medium rei*. This should be strongly insisted upon. When the question of the collaboration of believers and unbelievers in the temporal city arises, difficulties should not be underrated; nor can it be denied that some divergences admit of no solution, except those of good will, friendship, and toleration. For example, rational ethics may accept divorce, as a practice which, provided it is held within well-defined limits, and in no way delivered to the whimsicality of desires, has a part to play in the legal forms of marriage in a certain state or at a certain level of common morality. But Christianity has placed mankind in an existential condition in which marriage should be possessed of all its dignity. When complete, the dignity of marriage implies indissolubility. In a city made up of Christians and non-Christians, it will be up to political prudence to find a means of sanctioning the full dignity of Christian marriage without imposing upon non-Christians—upon people living in the order of simple natural law—difficulties that would be neither intelligible nor manageable. We should point out that since differences in the existential condition of mankind leave matters of justice totally unmodified, matters of justice will supply a large field of complete agreement between Christians and non-Christians. When a problem is one of strict justice, there is no conceivable discrepancy between the answer of rational ethics and that of Christian ethics. Accordingly, issues concerning strict justice make up a core of complete agreement between Christians and non-Christians. The various concessions and acts of toleration which are necessary can best be conceived as taking place around this core of strict agreement made up of answers to questions of strict justice.

We have seen that a moral philosophy that cannot take into consideration the existential condition of man is unequal to its task. Several examples have shown that it gives conditional answers where unconditional ones are expected. Such a moral philosophy has been properly described by Jacques Maritain as inadequate. It is inadequate, and unequal to its object, because all it knows are essences, whereas existential conditions need to be known when there is a question of seeing the truth about the right and the wrong in human use and of directing human action. Once the inadequacy of a purely natural ethics is recognized, we must choose between two conclusions: one is that there is no adequate moral philosophy; the other, that moral philosophy, which, if left alone, is inadequate, should be made adequate by some sort of union with theology. The latter view was proposed by Maritain in writings that aroused much opposition, much anger, and confusion. Opposition came not only from those who hold that moral philosophy can be adequate without owing anything to theology, but also from those who hold that moral philosophy cannot be rendered adequate, and must be purely and simply replaced by theology. The only adequate practical science would be theology. If the case is such, the question remains whether moral philosophy should still be taught and studied, with constant reminders of its inadequacy, or should be purely and simply replaced in academic programs by moral theology. The question is pedagogical, not epistemological.

Our own position is that a purely rational moral philosophy is essentially misleading. The choice is between a system holding that moral theology is the only true ethics and a system holding with Maritain that, besides moral theology, there is room for a "moral philosophy adequately taken." To be taken adequately, moral philosophy must receive some principles from theology. Moral philosophy adequately taken would be a subalternate science. That such an epistemological entity[8] as a moral philosophy adequately taken, and owing its adequacy to its subalternation to theology, is possible has been established by Maritain beyond doubt. The question that may still bother those who have followed Maritain's exposition is this: Is not a moral philosophy adequately taken a duplicate of moral theology? If it is such a duplicate, it would really be a system of moral theology disguised and, in all likelihood, distorted.

A potent argument is derived from the experience of an epistemological need. The study of ethics and of politics shows that many issues that cannot be treated without appeal to revealed truth have not, in fact, been studied, or have not been studied well, by theologians. The question now arises whether this deficiency is accidental or essential. Did the theologians fail to study these questions well just because the achievements of their science, like all human achievements, are incomplete, and because in theology as in any other field of knowledge the choice of the questions that are factually studied is exposed to the innumerable contingencies of intellectual and academic life? Or should it be said that the domain of ethics comprises questions that do not admit of treatment by theological methods but demand to be treated philosophically, even though moral philosophy, in order to be adequate to these subjects, may have to subalternate itself to theology?

I merely raise this question without attempting to answer it, or even to formulate it properly. Moral experience reveals the keenly felt need for investigation by an adequate moral philosophy. And we may suggest that in some cases of insuperable obscurity the trouble may arise from the fact that issues calling for philosophic analysis have been studied only according to theological methods. Considering the pitiful need for explanation that we experience with regard to vital issues (above all, marriage and sex life), the least that can be said is that the question is worth examining.

## The Timely Need for Moral Philosophy

Let us recall the general conclusion of the first chapter: the idea developed there was that, although action cannot wait, the understanding of right and wrong is subject to a law of slow progress. We do not know so much about the physical universe, and yet we have every good reason to guess that it is less mysterious than the universe of morality. In the meantime, it is perfectly reasonable to trust the answers supplied by the inclinations of just hearts and by the traditions in which such inclinations are embodied. Elaborating on the contrast between explanation and fulfillment, we remarked that in a way our inability to explain the rules of our actions is not a terrible disorder, for in matters of action what is essential is not explanation but fulfillment. Adequate fulfillment is possible as long as the true answer is supplied by the inclinations of right hearts. Our last remark, however, was that the fulfillment of a rule of human action, in order to be truly human, must be rational. Thus it cannot be said that explanation is of no relevance to fulfillment so long as the proper rule is had. Explanation contributes a significant modality to fulfillment.

Here, at the end of these reflections on the nature of moral philosophy, we wish to call attention to another aspect of the issue. Even though fulfillment is essential and explanation is not, and even though it is normal that the explanation of morality, as well as that of nature, should come into existence by slow progress, it is conceivable that circumstances should cause the need for explanation to be felt as a pressing one—stressing that if it is not satisfied fulfillment is endangered. Roughly, such seems to be the case with the societies of our time. People—and the younger ones in particular—seem to be particularly unwilling to abide by rules of action that they do not understand. With due allowance for the conjectural character of such comparisons, it seems reasonable to say that the people of our time are less willing than those of some other times to fulfill without understanding. This particularly strong demand for explanation, this particular reluctance to fulfill rules that are not explained, can be traced to two general facts. One is the breakdown of tradition. No doubt some societies are more disposed than others to abide by tradition. Now, it is tradition that proposes rules that have to be fulfilled whether they are understood or not. It is tradition that is supposed to conserve and to utter the rules that are established by the inclinations of just hearts without being, as yet, provided with a character of rational clarity. If the tradition is distrusted, people are reluctant to believe that the rule it proposes has been established by the inclinations of just hearts, and should be fulfilled even if it is not explained. So long as explanation has not come, nothing is left, and rules are likely to remain unfulfilled.

There is a second, and probably less important, factor: societies may be more or less eager for rationality as a result of unequal stages in the development of rational culture. Some might be tempted to say that minds in our societies are particularly eager for explanation because of the high development of scientific culture and because of all the scientific spirit embodied in the technological environment which is ours. Again, this factor is probably less significant than the general breakdown of tradition.

At all times and under all circumstances it is important to recall that explanation may not be considered a necessary condition for fulfillment. At all times and under all circumstances it is necessary to be ready to fulfill without understanding. Yet when the demand for explanation seems to be particularly pressing, the process of explanation should, in answer to such a demand, be carried out with particular zeal and a sense of urgency. It follows that the tasks proper to the moral philosopher are particularly significant and urgent in societies such as ours.

Considering the work commonly done in moral philosophy, let it be said that the first thing to be desired would be the ascertainment of the moral status of every proposition. Does an ethical rule enjoy a characteristic of natural evidence? Is it to be demonstrated? If it is neither self-evident nor demonstrated, all it guarantees is its agreement with the inclinations of just hearts. Because prudence alone can answer questions engaged in the determinations of contingency, we are tempted to forget that prudence can also answer general questions and supply general premises. In fact, it often happens that prudential answers, general in character, which are sufficient for the purpose of fulfillment, but not for that of explanation, are printed in a book side by side with demonstrated propositions which satisfy the demand for explanation. We should be clear about the difference.

Better judges will be able to say whether all this weighs in favor of a moral philosophy adequately taken, subalternated indeed to theology, but distinct from it. That philosophy, in all its parts, is thoroughly concerned with explanation is not in doubt. But perhaps theology, in its practical part, is concerned more with fulfillment than with explanation. This remains to be seen. What is clear is that an ardent development of explanation in the world of morality is an urgent need of our time.

# APPENDIX

# Extracts from Correspondence Between Yves R. Simon and Jacques Maritain

### SIMON TO MARITAIN, FEBRUARY 11, 1961

The present letter concerns difficulties raised by the reconsideration of the problems of practical knowledge, of which we spoke so often a quarter of a century ago. I would not take the liberty of asking you to help me in my new work on this subject were it not that I discuss some of your ideas. I cannot imagine myself publishing a discussion of your theories without first submitting it to you.

In the book *Practical Knowledge* that I am preparing I give much zealous attention and much space to the problem of "practically practical" versus "theoretically practical" science. I fully agree with all you say concerning the theoretical *mode* of moral philosophy. I might even go further than you in the direction of a theoretical interpretation of this science. (You notice that I avoid the word "speculative" which has come to be loaded with connotations of uncertainty. In the daily English of our time, speculative considerations are highly conjectural and amount to hardly more than guesswork.) In my opinion, moral philosophy is primarily designed to *explain* the things of morality, to answer theoretical questions, and if it contributes to the fulfillment of moral laws, it is essentially insofar as the *understanding* of what is morally right and wrong is of relevance to the truly human, that is, the intelligent fulfillment of the laws governing human action. But moral philosophy cannot carry out its task of explanation without considering, in the most essential fashion, the right and the wrong *use* of human powers, and

---

*By permission of the Yves R. Simon Institute, Mishawaka, Indiana, and the Cercle d'Etudes Jacques et Raïssa Maritain, Kolbsheim.*

because of this essential consideration of human use—a consideration entirely foreign to the natural philosophy of man—moral philosophy is a practical science in a proper sense, and is concerned with directing "from a distance" human action. In all other respects it is theoretical. How John of St. Thomas came to consider it a part of natural philosophy (the most un-Aristotelian view that can be imagined) is an accident that remains as unexplained to me today as it was in 1934.

Concerning the practically practical disciplines, I deliver my conclusion right away: they exist; they are irreducibly distinct both from theoretically practical sciences and from prudence; they are valuable and important, but they are not sciences. The last point, on which I disagree with the letter, if not with the deep intention, of *The Degrees of Knowledge*, calls for a qualification in the case of St. John of the Cross and in similar cases.

I notice that you do not *elaborate* on the scientific character of practically practical ethics. On p. 314 of the Phelan translation, I read "This is a science because . . . it nevertheless moves within the universal and the *raisons d'être* as within its proper object." Is this enough to give a discipline a scientific character? I refer to the definition of science that St. Thomas gets out of the *Posterior Analytics*. *Cognitio certa per causas* does not designate merely a discipline in which both certainty and explanation are found. It designates a discipline in which explanations are certain and certainties are explanatory. We find both certainty and explanation in history. It is perfectly certain that Napoleon was defeated at Waterloo on June 18, 1815. But the certainty of this fact does not convey the explanation of the same. Do we explain why Napoleon was defeated at Waterloo? Historians hardly do anything other than answer questions of the *why* type, and they do not always talk nonsense. But their explanations always are, in an essential way, unfinished; in the same essential way, they are uncertain. Because the defeat of Napoleon at Waterloo is an event engaged in contingency, it cannot be explained without a never-ending regression in the order of contingent causes, and this regression branches indefinitely many times. Then, how do we reasonably set a limit to our causal regressions, and how can we ever declare that an historical event has been satisfactorily explained? Notice that what is done in history is also constantly done in daily life. With regard to obviously contingent events we ask the question "Why did it happen?" and we often feel that it has been satisfactorily answered in a finite, and even small, number of words. By reflecting on these issues, I thought I discovered, quite a number of years ago, that the questions regarding contingent events which we consider satisfactorily answered, either in daily life or in historical work, are *practical questions*. There are such things as practical questions and there are such things as *practical explanations*. The practical questions are of the types "What ought we to do? What should we have done? What are we going to do?" Considering, for instance, the case of one who failed to accomplish his purpose, we ask *why* he failed. We look for an explanation of his failure, and a time may come when we quite reasonably hold that his failure has been explained. In truth, the question that we are asking amounts to this: "In order not to fail, what should he have done?" "In case someone else wants to accomplish a similar purpose, what should he do?" These are practical questions.

In your discussion of the practically practical sciences, you insisted on the practical character of the mode of conceptualization. Indeed, these "sciences" use practical ways of conceptualizing, but I suspect that their practical conceptualization corresponds to practical questions—a concept, a definition, are, in a way, an answer to a question—and that their *explanations* are practical.

If such is the case, practically practical disciplines, no matter how valuable and important they may be, are not sciences. Science, as a habitus of the theoretical intellect, is concerned with theoretical questions and is obliged to answer with certainty theoretical questions. The practically practical disciplines deal with practical explanations, and this would suffice to deny them the scientific character. Concerning certainty, I would say that it proceeds either from analysis into self-evident premises, or from the right inclination of the appetite. In the first case, we have a habitus of the theoretical intellect, a science, but it proceeds analytically and theoretically. This is the case with moral philosophy. In the second case, we have a habitus of the practical intellect, which proceeds synthetically and practically, and its name is prudence.

I alluded to a qualification to be made regarding St. John of the Cross or similar instances. As you pointed out, the unity of the theological habitus, which is not disrupted by the distinction of the theoretical and the practical, *a fortiori* is not disrupted by the distinction of the theoretically and the practically practical. The wisdom of St. John of the Cross remains a particular development of the theological habitus (*The Degrees of Knowledge*, p. 318), and insofar as it belongs to the theological habitus, you find in it a scientific character which is not found in the work of those whom we call moralists, in contradistinction to moral philosophers. You found in St. John of the Cross wonderful examples of concepts worked out according to a law that is practical, e.g., his concept of contemplation as a state of non-acting. "[St. John of the Cross] takes the point of view of mystical experience itself, and from this point of view, the suspension of every activity in the *human mode* appears to the soul as nonactivity. Not to move oneself, to cease from all particular operation, to be in supreme act of attentive and loving immobility, which is itself received from God—is this not *to do nothing*, not of course, in the ontological sense, but in the psychological and practical meaning of the word" (*The Degrees of Knowledge*, p. 327)? It is hardly possible to say more clearly that the question answered by the San Juanistic description of contemplation as a state of non-acting is not a theoretical question, i.e., a question of the "what are the things" type, but a question of the "what ought we to do, what shall we do, what should we have done" type, i.e., a practical question. The practically practical disciplines are not sciences because their explanations are practical explanations. If an objection is raised to the very concept of practical explanation, I would, as an old logician of analogy, answer by the following proportionality, in which x stands for practical explanation, x: theoretical explanation :: practical knowledge : theoretical knowledge.

Thus, the practically practical disciplines would be excluded from the realm of science by the nature of their explanations. The nature of explanation, whether theoretical or practical, would be anterior to the mode of conceptualization—an issue that you have treated so successfully. Then comes the question of certainty. Whatever the nature of their explanations, what is it that would give the practically practical disciplines the power to make themselves certain? As far as I know, the certainty of a discipline—and in order for a discipline to be scientific we need it to be certain *in its explanations*—results either from an analysis into axiomatic premises or from the fully dependable inclination of a heart in connaturality with the good. The first method of certainty is ruled out by the practical and synthetic mode of the disciplines under consideration. The second mode belongs to the virtues of the practical intellect and, since we are concerned with subjects involving the right or wrong use of free choice, to prudence. Now, for one thing, a certitude obtained "by way of inclination" never could be the certitude of a scientific explanation; for another, the examples that you give of non-philosophical moralists (*The Degrees of Knowledge*, p. 316), "Montaigne, Pascal, Nietzsche, Shakespeare, Racine, Baudelaire, Swift, Meredith, Balzac, Dostoevski," include a majority of men who, according to all appearances, did not possess the fullness of moral virtue that the certitude of prudence implies. I remember that at the time of your first publications, and of mine, on these subjects, I upheld the foolish idea—I do not know where I got it from—that in order to be a good observer of the world of morality, a man must possess the virtue of prudence. Against this you had several arguments, one of which was the just-quoted list of names. I was somewhat astonished to see that only a few lines after listing these names, you write (*The Degrees of Knowledge*, p. 316) ". . . the accuracy and depth of their views do not depend only upon their keenness of sight but also upon their idea of good and evil and the dispositions of their heart toward a sovereign good." What about the dispositions of the heart in the case of Montaigne or in that of Nietzsche?

To conclude, I wish to remark that, in all likelihood, what led you to attribute a scientific character to the practically practical disciplines was the theological example that lies at the center of all your inquiry. Again I go over our list of moralists. Several of them are literary creators, and the others do not show any inclination toward the systematic forms which are, in a great variety of ways and degrees, those of scientific thought. By calling his main work *Essays*, Montaigne lets the reader know that his expositions will not even submit to the rules of order that obtain in rhetoric. In good old French, a *"discours"* is supposed to be organized according to definite rules. An *"essai,"* on the contrary, does not need to be systematic at all. If Pascal had not died prematurely, his work would not be made of fragments; we have every reason to believe that it would be a well-organized book, but its organization would be that of a book of apologetics—still another branch of the theological habitus.

In spite of my badly limited competence, I could not afford to do without a discussion of your ideas on "moral philosophy adequately taken." You remember that I have always considered your theory favorably, and sometimes enthusiastically. I have no doubt that a moral philosophy which is not subordinated to theology cannot be existentially true. But a science of human conduct has to be existentially true, so that our choice is restricted to these two possibilities: either give up moral philosophy entirely, and trust theology with every scientific inquiry in the domain of morality, or adhere to your theory of moral philosophy adequately taken.

You may remember that a few months ago you were kind enough to read the long conclusion of a paper of mine on "Practical Wisdom."[9] In that conclusion I developed the idea that in practical matters the significant thing is not so much explanation as fulfillment. Every day we have to fulfill rules that have never been explained in airtight ways, and this can be done as long as knowledge by inclination formulates the rules of our action. In the conclusion of my discussion of these issues,[10] I intend to stress the importance of explanation in periods like ours, which are marked by a loss of faith in ethical traditions. It is mostly by tradition that the *inclinations of the just hearts* make their content known to the great number of men. If tradition breaks down and explanation is lacking, nothing is left. People prove unwilling to fulfill rules that no one can explain to them with rigor. This you vividly realize when you think of the writings of Bertrand Russell on sexual ethics and of their lasting influence. Things pertaining to marriage, sex, and purity are among the most obscure of the whole universe of morality. The criticism of Russell means that he sees no reason to fulfill difficult rules whose intelligible necessity he does not perceive. Thus I conclude that we live at a time when the explanation of things ethical has assumed a character of extreme importance and extreme urgency. Now, the first function of moral philosophy is not to ensure the fulfillment of ethical rules, but to *explain* these rules, and more generally everything that is non-contingent in the world of morality. I wonder if, from this consideration, I can draw an argument in favor of moral philosophy adequately taken as opposed to a situation in which moral theology would be the only science of morality. Am I entitled to say "We need explanation urgently; moral philosophy exists primarily for the sake of explanation"? As to theology, I am inclined to believe that it does not exist primarily for the sake of explanation, but for the sake of something else, whose exact nature I am not able to define. If it were established that theology, whether moral or not, exists primarily for the sake of something other than explanation, then my remaining doubts concerning the necessity of a moral philosophy adequately taken would vanish forever: for I do not doubt that we urgently need a science whose primary function is to bring forth the intelligible necessity of ethical rules.

## SIMON TO MARITAIN, FEBRUARY 15, 1961

I have reread my old (1934) *Critique de la connaissance morale* and compared it with what I am doing now on the subject of moral philosophy. This is what I discovered: in those years of my early youth, I laid strong emphasis on the function of moral philosophy as science designed to *direct human action*.[11] At the present time, my tendency is rather to view moral philosophy as a system of explanation which, though practical in a proper sense by reason of its consideration of *human use*, exists primarily for the sake of explaining the things of morality.[12] I might have been led to underrate the role that moral philosophy plays in the direction of human acts if I had not insistently remarked that in order to be truly human, as human as possible, fulfillment must be accompanied by explanation. In 1934, I put things in a slightly different way: then I said that, for the rationality of our actions, there ought to be an act of direction *at the level of intelligibility, which is that of moral philosophy.* This need for a correspondence between the level of understanding and the level of direction is a discovery. Clearly, if an act of direction did not take place at the level where moral philosophy carries out its explanations, moral philosophy would fail to contribute this rational mode which pertains in non-accidental fashion to the integrality of human acts. Thus, moral philosophy would be practical in a proper sense not only because it takes into consideration the *human use* of our abilities, but also because it has to contribute the intelligent way of fulfilling to the fulfillment of our rules of action.

## Maritain to Simon, February 22, 1961

Our difference about what I have called practico-practical science seems secondary to me. However, here are my reasons:

(1) I think that one must save for prudence alone the distinction of a knowledge directing human acts with *certainty* without being in any way a science.

(2) Of course, if one defines science as purely theoretical, you make your point. But I think that it would be begging the question and it is precisely the validity of this definition which I refuse to recognize.

(3) True, it is with practical explanations that the practico-practical sciences answer a practical question (which is not however totally individualized as in the case of prudence). However it suffices that these explanations be certain and proceed from *universal* and cogent *raisons d'être* for them to pertain to a science.

Some element of a theoretical nature is indeed implied there by the universality and cogency of the *raisons d'être*. The mode of conceptualization is practical; nevertheless *there is conceptualization*, and through concepts that are universal. Knowledge by connaturality permeates and governs this very universality (this implies that the subject possesses the virtue of prudence but not that his judgment is a prudential judgment bearing on a particular case in unique circumstances). Knowledge by connaturality also arouses in the mind these cogent reasons, and vitalizes them through experience. Such is the setting that causes me to speak of practico-practical science.

In brief, one has to *enlarge analogically* the notion of science. I reject your use of history as an analogical example—history is not a science because it does not formally employ universal *raisons d'être*. I would rather choose as an example (purely analogical and itself belonging to the strictly speculative order) our modern sciences of phenomena. These sciences do not correspond strictly to the Aristotelian concept of science because they are constantly changing.

(4) I cited Pascal, Montaigne, etc. . . . as moralists; I did not say that they all were *good* moralists or that they were exempt from error, or that they possessed prudence in the perfect state. It is enough that they had prudence in a rough shape (I speak here of the ones who were not exempt from errors). As for the inclinations of the heart toward *a* certain sovereign good (I did not say toward the Sovereign Good), these obviously played a role in the practical knowledge (more or less corrupted though real) that they had of things moral. The sovereign good of Nietzsche was not God but his own human grandeur.

I am very happy with our agreement over the notion of moral philosophy adequately considered. Your approach (through the necessity of *explaining* ethical rules and the things of morality) seems to me excellent and perfectly compatible with the other approach indicated in your second letter: to *direct human actions* at the level of intelligibility, which is that of moral philosophy. These two points of view are complementary and call for each another, and I think, as you do, that they are simultaneous.

(N.B.: The last practical judgment is distinct from the *imperium*. It does not say "Do this!" It says "Here is what is to be done!"). . . .[13]

## Simon to Maritain, March 8, 1961

It makes me feel very ashamed and unhappy to realize that, as foreseen, you spent so much time and energy commenting on my letter on practical knowledge. But what could I do? To be sure, publishing a discussion of your ideas without first having submitted my project to your judgment was out of the question. And to tell the whole truth, I guess that for you also there is something sweet about discussing again these subjects which, some thirty years ago, so often kept us happy together, in spite of the things which were coming and of which we were so aware.

Our divergences may boil down to setting forth, in slightly different ways, identical views on practically practical science. (I notice that, contrary to your usage of 1932, you constantly speak of "practico-practical" science. It had always been my understanding that this word, of late coinage and used only by "scholastico-scholastics" of the pre-Maritain generations, refers only to cognitions whose practical character is fully determinate, down to the last contingencies of individual action. Prudence alone would be "practico-practical." This was made clear by a footnote of *Critique de la connaissance morale*, page 81, where I declare that a discipline termed practically practical still belongs to speculativo-practical knowledge. Of course, I am strongly in favor of the adverbs of manner, whose grammatical nature suffices to make it clear that we are concerned with a *mode*, a *way*, of knowing.)

At the beginning of your letter, you write, as if this were a subject of disagreement between us, that prudence is the only cognition which directs human acts with certainty and is not a science in any way. Yet this is also what I hold, with particular firmness, when I maintain that the practically practical disciplines are not sciences.

I think, as you do, that if science is defined as purely theoretical, the whole issue is settled by a *petitio principii*. But the fellow who begged precisely this question has a name greater than mine. His name, or rather his surname, is John of St. Thomas. Only a few weeks ago I was entirely ready to follow you on the subject of the practically practical science—as well as on so many other subjects! My present doubts concern neither the existence nor the significance of the practically practical disciplines, but exclusively their scientific character. These doubts came to my mind as I became more aware of the following difficulties:

(1) The "explanatory certainty" of the practically practical disciplines concerns *practical* explanations. Now, whereas a practical mode of conceptualization seems to me compatible with the scientific character of a discipline, it also seems to me that a discipline loses its scientific character as soon as whatever it explains is explained only in a practical sense. I see a world of difference in this respect between conceptualization and explanation. By considering scientific disciplines whose mode of conceptualization is practical, you have, on the one hand, shown how far the concept of scientific interpretation (with the theoretical connotations that it inevitably conveys) can go in enlightening the obscure, difficult, and historically neglected subject of practical knowledge. Friend, believe me: I would not have worked steadily on the subject of practical knowledge from the schoolboyish days of *Critique* until the present days, which may not be followed by many more on this planet, if my desire to cast every possible bit of intelligibility on the problems of action was not very ardent. Again, the man who said that there is no such thing as a practical science has a name much uglier than mine (Poinsot), but even in Heaven I do not hope ever to obtain such a lovely surname as his—unless especially clever angels derive something from my faithfulness to your teachings.

On May 19, 1922, the Feast of St. Yves, a dear friend who now is Bishop of Quimper presented me with *Art and Scholasticism*. (The inscription remarked that he was a scholastic and that I was an artist; true, I was still writing poetry, but only a few months later I discovered that poetic composition was a thing for which I did not have the slightest suspicion of talent.) And, thus, ever since the days following the Feast of St. Yves, 1922, the intellectual habitus have been for me, thanks to you, familiar as well as beloved companions. Of these five habitus, three belong to the theoretical intellect and two to the practical intellect. John of St. Thomas is wrong when he considers that the line of demarcation is constituted by the defining features of science, so that, properly speaking, there could not be such a thing as a practical science. (*Log*, 2. q. 27, a. i and a. 4). Father Phelan, who likes to say that the great commentators of the Renaissance nearly understood St. Thomas, but that you were the first to understand him better than nearly, would enjoy this remark. Remote ages will praise you not only for having vindicated the concept of practical science against our beloved teacher, John of St. Thomas, but also for having struggled hard to carry the effects of scientific understanding as far as possible into the domain of practice. My own opinion is that the line of demarcation is not constituted, as John of St. Thomas believes, by the defining features of science. There exist, in a proper sense, practical sciences. But I am strongly inclined to hold that disciplines that exercise explanatory certainty *with regard to practical explanations alone* are not on the scientific side of the line of demarcation. They belong to the habitus of the practical intellect, and back we are to May 19, 1922, the Feast of St. Yves.

Fittingly, views relative to explanation are supplemented by views relative to certainty. The certainty of the practically practical disciplines does not proceed from an analysis into axioms, but from the righteous inclination of the heart. This also places us on the non-scientific side of the demarcation line and again we are back to May 19, 1922. It was a great day.

I am seriously troubled by the difficulties you raise concerning the last practical judgment and command. In a long article, "Introduction to the Study of Practical Wisdom," just published by *The New Scholasticism*,[14] I speak all the time as if "command" and "ultimate practical judgment" were one and the same. The question is still more important in a discussion of the *obedience due to man* (in my recently completed book *General Theory of Authority*, in which I answer objections raised by Arthur E. Murphy). I suppose that the solution is this: I call "ultimate practical judgment" an *oratio imperativa* (I learned from your *Formal Logic* that not all "speeches" are propositions; some of them are imperative speeches). By "last practical judgment" I mean the last proposition *with* the assent that actuates it into a judgment: "Here is what is to be done!" I would call "command" the non-propositional speech by which I order myself to do the thing which, according to the last proposition, ought to be done! "Do this!" Of the command, I would not hesitate to say that it is as practical as action itself. After having given much thought to your remark, I am tempted to conclude that I still can say the same of the ultimate practical judgment. This judgment, because it is the completely determinate form of the action, is as practical as action itself.

There has been a misunderstanding between us on the subject of history. If history is mentioned in my letter, it is not for the purpose of extending the notion of science analogically. I just wanted to show that the definition of science requires certainties that are explanatory and explanations that are certain. Now, historical explanations are not certain, and historical certainties are not explanatory. Thus, no question of "analogical extension."

To conclude this inconclusive discussion, I wish to express my belief in practically practical *disciplines*; I think that they occupy a very important place among the productions of the human mind. The only thing of which I am not sure is that they are *sciences*. After all, a discipline does not need to be a science to be important. If the position that appears probable to me turns out to be true, there would be no science and no habitus between moral philosophy and prudence. This vast region would be cultivated by disciplines that cannot attain the rank of habitus. Why should this not be the case? Such a vision would agree nicely with the Aristotelian picture of the five intellectual habitus.

I was very happy with your encouragement concerning moral philosophy adequately taken. As I work on the subject of "fulfillment versus explanation" I am making discoveries that may be of some significance. I had always assumed that the purpose of Socrates was primarily the understanding, the explanation, of moral affairs. But a passage in St. Augustine's *City of God* (Book 8, Chap. 3) seems to mean that his primary concern was the *content* of moral life. Contrary to the interpretation we received from Nietzsche, Sorel, and a few others, the Athenians would not have tried a "rationalist" who endangered their traditions by developing in the youth a taste for the rational vindication of the rules of action. Rather, they would have defended the old set of rules against the new ones proposed by Socrates. This seems to be St. Augustine's interpretation, and I am greatly interested in it for the following reason. You remember the passage from the beginning of the *Ethics* where Aristotle declares with insistence that people whose judgment is upset by passion cannot follow a course in ethics properly. He goes so far as to say that even if they understand, they miss the goal, for the goal, in practical matters, is not understanding, but action. Now, the ten books of the *Ethics* are full of things that it is good to understand even if conduct is not improved. To keep unwelcome auditors from his classroom, Aristotle uses an argument I consider incompatible with his views on the intrinsic excellence of theoretical perfection. But what about this hypothesis? He was addressing a fraction of the opinion which, in line with Socrates (as understood by St. Augustine), considered that the moral philosopher was altogether concerned with rules to be fulfilled. There would remain something paradoxical about Aristotle's making the statement that the student in ethics purely and simply misses his goal if his fulfillment of moral rules is not improved, but this paradox would become more tolerable in view of an historical situation that Nietzsche and the others have taken out of the picture. Do you remember the article by Boutroux on Socrates as founder of ethical science? It remains extremely interesting, but, if Boutroux were right, ethics would not be a science in the sense of Aristotle; rather, it would be a dialectical system, using, as becomes dialectic, the opinions of the elders in lieu of axioms. Again, it could not be said that the primary purpose of moral philosophy is the explanation of moral affairs. If Aristotle had any doubts on the subject, such doubts could easily be traced to the lack of a clear theory of knowledge by inclination.

### NOTES

1. Chap. 8, pp. 310–51. See also Yves R. Simon, *Critique de la connaissance morale* (Paris: Desclée De Brouwer, 1934), pp. 100–13.
2. (London: Allen & Unwin, 1930).
3. See *Material Logic of John of St. Thomas*, p. 593n34: "Conceptualization is practical and synthetic because the final purpose is not unqualified explanation—i.e., explanation in terms of essential necessity—but *practical explanation*, i.e., explanation in terms of human action and by way of answers to the questions 'what ought we to do?' 'what should we have done?' again 'what shall we do?' "

4. See *Degrees of Knowledge*, p. 318: "And the very clear distinction that must be acknowledged between them ('them,' i.e., theology as understood by St. Thomas and the practically practical science found in St. John of the Cross) does not go so far as to make two specifically different *habitus* of them; for the practical science in question should be considered as a particular development of the theological *habitus*."

5. Ibid., p. 316.

6. For additional discussion of the problem of practically practical science, see the letter to Jacques Maritain of February 11, 1961, pp. 100–106.

7. See Yves R. Simon, "Philosophie Chrétienne: Notes Complémentaires," *Etudes Carmélitanes*, 19 (1934), 107–19; *Critique de la connaissance morale*, chap. 8; "The Rationality of the Christian Faith," *Thought*, 21 (1956–1957), 495–508: and the letter to Maritain, February 11, 1961, pp. 100–106, below.

8. The epistemology of the question, in terms of a highly elaborate theory of scientific objectivity, is found in Maritain's *On Christian Philosophy* and in his *Science and Wisdom*.

9. See the section "Fulfillment and Explanation" in chap. 1, above.

10. See the section in this chapter on "The Timely Need for Moral Philosophy."

11. P. 87.

12. Ibid., p. 92.

13. Translated, with Maritain's approval, by Paule Y. Simon.

14. Chap. 1, above.

# 4

# From the Science of Nature to the Science of Society

### The Emergence of Social Science

THERE IS SOMETHING PARADOXICAL about our attitude toward social science. We would never question the extreme difficulty of any problem pertaining to the critique of scientific knowledge. Further, we have every good reason to believe that the things pertaining to society are more obscure than the things pertaining to nature. Yet we allow such issues as the object, method, and functions of the social sciences to be decided, quietly and painlessly, by dogmatic utterances, syllabi, postulations and semi-magical formulas.

The truth is that we have almost lost the hope of establishing with certainty the principles of social science. Now, when rational principles are lacking, the organization of knowledge depends entirely upon the consensus of the experts. Academic gentlemen, all of whom would dislike being confronted with a new era of doubt, have come to agree on some basic propositions to be used in lieu of axioms. Thus, social science is going through a *scholastic period*, for *scholasticism* as opposed to *science* is a system in which conventions faithfully adhered to by academic authorities assume the role of principles.

The concept of social science, as it is commonly interpreted, is something comparatively new. It would be presumptuous to assign the date of its first appearance; yet it can be said that it did not enjoy popularity until late in the eighteenth century.[1]

From then on it accomplishes quick progress; by 1830 it has won a position of overwhelming importance. Such success is explained to a large extent by an obvious and loudly proclaimed relation between the newly shaped theory of social science and the theory of physics which had been firmly established for some time. In order to know what we are talking about when we speak of social science, we must keep in mind the pattern after which it was first constructed. What are the characteristics of the physical system in which the founders of social science saw the archetype of all scientific treatment?

1. Physical science, such as the early social researchers saw it, is related more to a demiurgical ambition than to a contemplative ideal. Clearly, our knowledge of nature admits of two directions. It may be so conceived as to find its end in itself, in its own perfection, in the glory of truth. And it may be so conceived as to give man greater power over nature through the prediction of events. The ways determined by these two purposes do not necessarily coincide, and history shows that they often diverge.

At the dawn of Greek culture, the story of Thales[2] illustrates the theoretical or contemplative ideal which was to prevail among the Greeks. Thales, a philosopher and astronomer, was despised by business-minded neighbors because, they said, a man of science cannot gain much wealth. But astronomical observation gave him a chance to let his detractors learn more about what science can do. He foresaw a large crop of olives and rented all the olive-presses of the region. When harvest time came, farmers had to accept the monopoly prices that he exacted of them for subletting the presses. Thus, he was in a good position to maintain that a physicist can make money if only he cares to.

The contemplative ideal exalted by the Greeks remains predominant throughout the Middle Ages. It is at the time of the Renaissance that demiurgical ambitions take hold of scientific minds.[3] Such ambitions are expressed by Bacon and by Descartes in terms never forgotten. They pervade the modern science of nature.

2. The system used as a pattern for the science of society is a mathematical interpretation of nature. Among the many impli-

cations of this epistemological feature, one is of particular relevance to the present inquiry: if nature is treated mathematically, finality is excluded, more or less consistently, from its interpretation. There are no final causes in mathematics. Things that have been processed by mathematical abstraction are not desirable, no matter how desirable their knowledge may be.[4] Nature, as read by mathematicians, is deprived of goodness and of love.

3. Let us now consider the relation of physical science to society. Of particular significance is the fact that the science of nature worked out by the men of the Renaissance and their followers is steadily communicable, not only in terms of essential possibility (which would hold for all demonstrative knowledge), but also in a factual sense. The meaning of this remark is explained by the familiar contrast between the social behavior of science and that of philosophy. Philosophers are famous for their disagreements. It is excusable on the part of the layman to draw skeptical conclusions from this everlasting disorder, but the philosopher who likewise concludes that philosophy is impossible or uncertain shows that he has not understood how large the discrepancy may be, in the works of the mind, between essential and factual possibilities. The difficulties of philosophic research are great, and when, after many years spent on a question, we are so lucky as to master some aspect of the answer—when we know for sure that the proposition expressing this aspect of the answer is true and fully established, that there cannot be any leak in the demonstration, that the necessity of the assent is absolute—we still expect very few people, if any, to follow the demonstration and to commune with us in assenting to the conclusion. There is not any essential reason why those philosophic propositions which are fully demonstrated should not be unanimously accepted; but the purely incidental factors which interfere with the communication of philosophic truth are common and so inescapable that, until the end of the world, philosophic sciences will be, in terms of facts, disciplines of narrowly restricted communicability.

As to the science of nature prompted by the Renaissance, experience shows that men able to master it, or some parts of it, are not exceedingly few in the educated section of society;

among them there is a degree of consensus never achieved by the students of philosophy. A multitude of physical propositions is commonly accepted by physicists; and society is not short of proficient students of physics.

The demiurgical character of our physical science and its privilege of steady communicability combine in such a way as to produce an unprecedented relation between man and the physical world. The description of an example, which may well afford to be imaginary, may constitute a sufficient exposition of this combined operation and of the resulting state of affairs.

In spite of the good work done by our physicians, surgeons, biologists, and chemists, we cannot yet say that we know how to treat many forms of cancer. Now, so much good work has been done in the last generations for the treatment of the most stubborn diseases that we shall not be surprised if within a short time we hear that methods for the treatment of cancer have been used with complete success in an impressive number of cases. We all hope to see the day when a few hypodermic or intravenous injections suffice in most instances to free a human organism from such a dreaded disease. This happy day may come soon, it may come late, and it may never come. What matters for the present discussion is that we are able to set forth definite connections between the discovery of a specific remedy for cancer and happenings of great human significance.

If the discovery is genuine, it will quickly gain general recognition; within a few months or at most a few years it will obtain the unanimous assent of medical men all over the civilized world. Such a process of communication could not conceivably be prevented, postponed, or slowed down except by some great disaster. A second step will take place with almost equal inevitability: as soon as the medical authorities of the world are convinced that cancer can be effectively treated (or prevented) by the use of existent medicines, these medicines will be produced in amounts proportionate to the need. With the possible exception of a few remote islands, they will be available wherever wanted. Application will follow upon availability, and cancer will decline as did smallpox, yellow fever, and tuberculosis. Thus, in the relation of man to a common disease we perceive a factual link between knowledge and these developments: communication of scientific propositions, application of technical formulas to physical nature, and actual transformation of the world. It is not contended that these connections happen infallibly; in order that they be of high significance it suffices that they should hold in many or in most cases. Tuberculosis no longer is a major concern in technically advanced societies. Likewise, we shall no longer be badly worried about cancer when we know that it often can be healed or prevented by a few shots. Roughly: discovering the significant relation is all we need to ensure the actual promotion of human welfare. As soon as a new fragment of applicable science is available, society takes care of the application. True, there have been sad cases in which, for a long time, only a small part of mankind enjoyed the beneficial effects of a scientific progress. But, as society becomes more technological in its structure and its habits, the world-transforming decisions contained in the newly established formulas of natural science are enforced more speedily and more thoroughly. In a number of cases it can safely be said that major difficulties are over as soon as the phase of scientific discovery has been successfully concluded. Nothing so closely similar to salvation through knowledge alone has ever been experienced.

Unfortunately the salvation procured by the science of nature is so incomplete that disappointment is a constant experience for the scientific man. Is there a way out of a persistent wretchedness which is made more intolerable by its co-existence with inebriating success?

Here, the image of a science of society patterned after the science of nature could enter the scene. The domain of salvation through knowledge would then comprise, over and above our relation to physical things, the whole universe of social relations. Servitude, exploitation, destitution, and war would fall under the power of science. Hope for the end of exploitation would have as good a foundation as hope for the end of cancer. A good part of the problem of evil would be virtually solved. Such a vision attained a climax of intensity about a century ago; the best proof that social thinkers are still haunted by it is the resentment that fills their souls. We often read in works of popular philosophy as well as in scholarly journals that our mechanical engineers have done their duty and that our social engineers have not done theirs. The social engineer is a gentleman in charge of transforming society through the application of scientific formulas. As compared with those colleagues of his who deal with mechanics, he finds himself at a disadvantage. It is not enough to say that his task is more difficult.

Between physical and social causality the difference is such that the concept of engineer simply does not admit of being transferred from the physical to the social order. The undine, the zombie, and the social engineer are so many beings of reason with no foundation in the real world.[5] All this is granted by many who still fail to see what a deep reconsideration the concept of science calls for when we move from the world of nature to the world of society.

The concept of social engineering, whatever its relation to reality may be, seems a safe approach to the kind of scientific form that social objects require. A social engineer would be possible if it were not for the particular features of social causality. Now, these features matter not only in the phase of application (engineering) but also in the phase of understanding. If social engineering is impossible, so is any science which postulates that a natural system of causality controls social relations.

## Practical Knowledge of Social Science

Let us now go farther back in intellectual history. Again, it is not until late in the eighteenth century that the concept of a social science shaped after the pattern of physics got hold of scholarly opinion. What did the human mind do about social processes prior to this modern attempt?

Think of Plato, Aristotle, the Stoics, the Epicureans, St. Augustine, the Schoolmen, and the political scientists of the Renaissance. Their studies of society, which are still among the most valuable products of social thought, always take place in the context of a practical knowledge. The purpose of Aristotle in his writings on the family and the state is practical in the strict sense. As known, he divided sciences into the theoretical, the productive, and the practical. Productive sciences (e.g., architecture) can be termed practical without impropriety;[6] but politics is one of those sciences that are practical in a distinguished sense, for they direct the action of man precisely considered as human agent. Practical sciences, as distinct both from the theoretical and from the productive ones, are concerned with right choice in human acts. Politics is altogether concerned with the proper use of man's freedom in community life.

In sharp contrast with earlier approaches, the social science of modern times generally claims to be independent of ethical concerns. Its theorists hold that such independence is an essential condition for its objectivity, for its scientific character, and ultimately for the effective control of man over history. They concede that a teacher of social science cannot be forbidden to voice his preferences and value-judgments: whether he should or not is a pedagogical issue to be decided with due consideration for the circumstances; but pedagogical issues concern the teacher and his students, not the science that is taught and learned; value-judgments remain foreign and extrinsic to scientific analysis. In order to be objective and scientific in our approach to the laws of society we should set aside whatever we know or believe concerning the right and the wrong, just as we refrain from evaluating, in terms of right and wrong, thermodynamic or magnetic phenomena. It is perhaps at this point that the influence of the physical pattern upon social science is the most decisive. Max Weber[7] calls *Wertfreiheit* (literally, freedom from value) the epistemological feature that we are describing. The American translators of Weber render *Wertfreiheit* by "ethical neutrality." Another good translation would be "irrelevance of value-judgments." The theory of social science, in our time, is dominated by the postulate that value-judgments are irrelevant. A scholar who questions this postulate endangers his reputation; he will be accused, in the most distinguished academic circles, of ignoring the elementary requirements of the scientific attitude. True, such personal abuse is less irritating and less important than the cheap certitude enjoyed, as an effect of uncritical belief, by most social scientists and by their followers. To proclaim the irrelevance of value-judgments without having at least attempted an explanation of what is meant by value and by value-judgment is a striking example of the scholastic dogmatism which today interferes with the progress of social science. In fact, few expressions used by philosophers convey such a tangle of confused postulations as "value-judgment."

The origin and general meaning of these postulations are described by Professor Gilson in humorous sentences. Addressing the "apprentice in realistic philosophy," he cautions him against values. "Thus, it is necessary to keep away, by all means, from all speculations about 'values,' for values are nothing else but transcendentals that parted from being and endeavor to substitute for being."[8] The concept of value, as commonly understood in epistemology, is essentially idealistic. Accordingly, the so-called value-judgments are not supposed to express what things are: they spring from within myself. In the philosophy of Kant, judgments of ethical value arise from the core of the rational nature, from the core of human reason. On lower levels of philosophic theory value-judgments are accounted for by the operation of instincts and emotions.

The idealistic notions of value and value-judgment are important parts of a cosmic and metaphysical picture commonly associated with the scientific interpretation of experience. Convergent influences of scientific imagery and philosophic indoctrination have filled our minds with a dualistic expression of reality. This dualism is not exactly that of Descartes, though it owes much to it. A universe made of extension and motion is mysteriously confronted with consciousness. It is a non-teleological universe: again, a mathematical interpretation of nature is necessarily ignorant of final causes. But a world that is both real and non-teleological is meaningless. It is a tale told by an idiot, signifying nothing. No logos dwells in the universe of mechanism; it does not have any idea of its own. Man attempts an escape from meaninglessness by breathing words into things, but these man-uttered words never become the forms and souls of things; even when our effort to break away from nonsense is greatest, they remain mere value-judgments, in sharp contrast with judgments of reality. Current views on judgments of value follow from a general philosophy in which mechanism and idealism combine; these views are not any more scientific or less philosophic than this philosophy; they do not derive any power from the weight that belongs to positive propositions, for such weight is not theirs; they are just as arbitrary as idealism, mechanism, and any combination of these two.

In his celebrated paper on the postulate of *Wertfreiheit* (ethical neutrality, irrelevance of value-judgments),[9] Max Weber refers to the theory that historical trends supply transitions from facts to values. This suggestion must be carefully discussed. If we notice that a trend has prevailed over a large part of society and for a long time, shall we infer, from its sheer prevalence in these dimensions of social existence, that some excellence belongs to this trend, although the connection may still not be clearly intelligible? In the last fifty years the divorce rate has increased considerably, especially in societies characterized by readiness to welcome technical progress and to give up the traditional ways of life. Should it be said that the trend, by the very fact of its persistence, takes over a value in terms of rightness and progress? If this were the case, the divorce rate, other things being equal, should not decline, and the eccentrics who remain faithful to the principle of strict monogamy should be blamed for refusing to cooperate in the progress of mores. Whenever such inferences are drawn, it is easy to recognize the operation of the postulated principle that the law of mankind is one of inescapable progress. This law is supposed to be so strict as to tolerate no deviation of any considerable size or duration; as soon as a process assumes the character of a trend, one may be sure that the benevolent genius of history is at work. Clearly, such transmutation of facts into values proceeds from a mythological theory of the fact. It is not a solution to the problem of the relation between fact and value.

This problem may be considered from another angle. There is such a thing as an empirical apprehension of trends, which cannot lead to any value-judgment unless the least scientific alchemy is allowed, as in the example just used, to work its miracle. But there is also such a thing as a rational consideration of regularities, which may let us know something of an essence and of its identity with a tendency. If we use our intelligence to interpret regularities, circumscribe essences, penetrate them—no matter how exhaustively—observe adjustments, adaptations, successes and failures, the idealistic construct of the value-judgment fades away. A seed of corn grows into an adult plant of corn with remarkable regularity; is it so hard to understand that this is not just a matter of chance, and that you could not expect a seed of wheat, or a gold coin, to grow into a plant of corn with anything like the regularity displayed by corn seeds in spite of larvae, birds, floods, and dry weather? If we are able to understand that there are natures in nature, that natures are tendencies and that human nature is no exception, it should not be so extremely difficult to realize that the observation of men's behavior can teach us a few things about the tendencies of human nature and about what is good for man. Shall we speak of human nature? This expression, provided it is free from idealistic implications, is legitimate and necessary.[10] In the celebrated passage in which he shows what principles should be followed in the division of the natural law,[11] St. Thomas gives a simple and convincing demonstration of a transition from facts, metempirically considered, to values realistically understood. To set in order the multiple precepts contained in the unity of the natural law, let us watch human tendencies to discover, if we can, their relations of anteriority and posteriority. "The order," he says, "of the precepts of the natural law corresponds to the order of human inclinations." There are tendencies that man has in common with all things, such as the tendency to keep existing, to persevere in being. Suicide is contrary to natural law in the deepest and most radical sense. It goes against a tendency that springs from what is deepest in man and in all things, being.

> For there is in man, first of all, an inclination to good in accordance with the nature which he has in common with all substances, inasmuch, namely, as every substance seeks the preservation of its own being, according to its nature; and by reason of this inclination, whatever is a means of preserving human life, and of warding off its obstacles, belongs to the natural law.

Then there are tendencies that man has in common with other animals, such as those relative to generation.

> Secondly, there is in man an inclination to things that pertain to him more specially, according to that nature which he has in

common with other animals; and in virtue of this inclination those things are said to belong to the natural law which nature has taught to all animals, such as sexual intercourse, the care of the offspring and so forth.

Finally some tendencies pertain to what is distinctively human in man, the life of reason.

> Thirdly, there is in man an inclination to good according to the nature of his reason, which nature is proper to him. Thus man has a natural inclination to know the truth about God, and to live in society; and in this respect, whatever pertains to this inclination belongs to the natural law: e.g., to shun ignorance, to avoid offending those among whom one has to live, and other such things.

Let us dare to suggest that the needed information of social science may require, as an antecedent step, the reconsideration of physical knowledge itself. The first object of our understanding is the intelligibility of nature, and every intellection, no matter how abstract, remains in some way connected with the things that were understood first. Nature supplies our intellect with a universal pattern of intelligible reality. Correspondingly, the science of nature remains, in a way, the pattern after which we conceive all sciences or at least all sciences of the real world. The mathematical interpretation of nature, with all its beauty and all its utility, supplies our knowledge of the real with a deceitful pattern if it is erected into what is not, viz., a philosophy of physical reality. A new effort to ascertain the principles of physical science may be the first thing required for the needed reinterpretation of the science whose object is human society.

## Nature and Use in Social Science

The influence of the patterns supplied by natural science never went unopposed. Social scientists have been struggling indefatigably for the autonomy of their discipline; they dedicated much zeal and ingenuity to the search for a method strictly adjusted to social facts. As recalled in the foregoing, the study of society, prior to the modern era, was commonly engaged in systems of judgments about the right and the wrong. But once the influence of the physical pattern had been felt, few social thinkers went so far as to suspect that an approach in terms of right and wrong could be implied in the autonomous structure that they were looking for. Few stopped to think that the intelligibility of an act may change according as this act is right or wrong. To be sure, such change never takes place as long as things are considered within the system of nature and natural causality. But it cannot be taken for granted that the causality and the intelligibility which pertain to social facts are of such character that differences in ethical meanings leave them unmodified. A chemical process, considered as event of nature, offers exactly the same intelligibility whether it is used for purposes of healing or for purposes of murder. But when a social process is considered as social, as engaged in the distinct system of causation which belongs to society, it is impossible to assume, without further ado, that intelligibility is never modified by the meanings of things and occurrences in terms of morality. In our endeavor to determine the autonomous structure of social science, one major issue is the question of whether the *social* nature of a process is such as to modify the forms of intelligibility that scientific research purposes to bring forth. Notice, at this point, that the idealistic interpretation of value-judgments prevented many minds from noticing that the moral, social, and political literature of all times is made principally of investigations and descriptions of facts. In the older products of social thought propositions structured by "is" are incomparably more numerous than propositions structured by "ought." It looks very much as if a book aimed at the establishment of rules for the welfare of man and society should contain a heavy load of case-histories, records of general facts, and comparative observations. Let us suppose, for instance, that an elementary analysis of human finalities—which analysis, as recalled, consists in the intelligent reading of factual occurrences and cannot consist in anything else—has shown that family life and the stability of the home are better for man than individualistic isolation. When such a principle is established, an investigation of facts, which may have to be very extensive, is still necessary in order to determine what circumstances favor the good of family life and oppose the evils of individualistic hopelessness. Even though we may rarely use the grammatical structure of normative expression, such inquiries into the fact are constantly guided by principles concerning the right and the wrong in human actions. In these investigations the role of judgments about the right and the wrong is not incidental, not extrinsic, not superadded; it is intrinsically relevant. The context is such that the fact, in order to be understood, in order to reveal the intelligibility which it possesses in precisely such a context, demands to be interpreted, explicitly or implicitly, directly or indirectly, loudly or silently, in relation to what is good and what is bad for man and society.

We have reached the point where the problem of *Wertfreiheit* admits of accurate statement. There is a context in which the consideration of acts, in order to be intelligent, needs to be interpretative in terms of right and wrong.[12] The question now is whether social science exercises its acts in a context of this nature. Seen from a certain angle, human facts present such an objective constitution that the perception of their relation to the right and the wrong is essential to their understanding. Does social science consider things from this angle?[13] The theory of ethical neutrality holds that it does not. What we need is a criterion for the identification of those contexts in which the intelligibility of facts includes a reference to human values.

Our suggestion is that the key to the answer lies in the relation between the concept of *nature* and the concept of *use*. As long as we are concerned with natures—human nature not being excluded—the consideration of the ethically right and wrong is plainly irrelevant. But when the human use of natures pertains intrinsically to the intelligible constitution of the object, the principle of ethical neutrality, contrary to the claims of its upholders, conflicts with the requirements of objectivity.

The things that man makes use of are good or bad according to the condition of their natures and independently of the use made of them. This is a platitude of inexhaustible significance. One can make a good use of a good horse and a good use of a poor horse and a bad use of a poor horse and a bad use of a good horse. One may, just as well, make a good use of a good memory and a good use of a poor memory, etc. At the very center of human action, one may make a good use of a strong will and a good use of a weak will and a bad use of a weak will and a bad use of a strong will. As long as the intelligible structure which is being considered is that of a nature, use remains extrinsic, moral quality remains incidental, and the principle of ethical neutrality holds. In the works of Aristotle psychology is nothing else than the upper part of natural science. It is conversant with the nature of the soul, of its powers and operations; it has nothing to do with the good or bad use that men make of their senses, their memory, their imagination, their intellect, and their will. If it ever considers a question of integrity, the integrity considered amounts merely to the entirety or plentitude of a nature. Psychology, a part of the science of nature, ignores the unique kind of plenitude which consists of conformity between the freedom of man and the rule of his action. On the contrary, the studies of facts which, as recalled, play a great part in ethics and in political philosophy center in the use that men make of things and of themselves. The principle of ethical neutrality holds in psychology. (Thus, insights into the right and wrong use of memory are entirely extrinsic and altogether obnoxious in a psychological study of memory.) The principle of ethical neutrality does not hold in the factual investigations pursued by the moralist and the political philosopher. (Thus, a moralist who studies memory does not abstract from the good or bad use that man makes or is likely to make of it. From his standpoint, memory appears as the power of realizing the wretchedness of an existence that cannot endure without entering into the unknown and disappearing into nothingness; such a power demands to be healed and strengthened by the virtue of hope.) Does the social scientist resemble the theoretical philosopher and like him consider natures and natural integrity? Or does he resemble the moralist, who, even when he deals with facts and utters no "ought," remains intrinsically concerned with human use? This may be the decisive statement of the problem.

To increase the chances of finding the answer, we must clarify our notions concerning the causes of social events. But in such a connection epistemological inquiry is commonly hampered by prevailing ideas about causality. We all received from our early philosophic education the notion that causality implies the qualitative and existential relations which define a deterministic scheme in natural science. Any process at variance with the laws of a deterministic scheme is uncritically deemed to evidence a lack of causality; it is interpreted in terms of contingency and chance, and its incompletely "causal" character is traced to some deficiency, some inachievement, some lack of determination. The consequences are obvious: since there is no science of the accident, we cannot even hope for the constitution of a social science without postulating that social processes are brought about according to the laws of a so-called deterministic system. It follows that the science of society is held to be a study of natures, of natural events, of natural growth and decrease, and of natural plenitude. Such a science is unconcerned with use and consequently requires an attitude of ethical neutrality. The whole question was begged when it was granted, perhaps carelessly, that a process at variance with the deterministic pattern is necessarily marked by a lack of causal determination. The basic mistake was our willingness to be satisfied with cheap postulates about the issue of freedom.[14] The whole framework of the epistemological problem changes when we come to realize, in spite of common prejudice, that the free will is not less but more of a cause than the univocally determinate nature; that freedom originates in an excess rather than in a lack of natural necessity; that a free process is superdeterminate rather than indeterminate; that freedom is an intense, excellent, and overflowingly powerful mode of causality; that it is not accident or chance, and that the mystery of free events, in spite of appearances, is opposite in character to the mystery of chance. As soon as the theory of freedom is cleared of indeterministic misinterpretations it becomes possible to consider coldly the question whether the object of social science comprises, over and above facts pertaining to natural determination, some facts pertaining to the use that human freedom makes of itself and of the natural powers subjected to it.

There is no question of claiming that the socially relevant behavior of man is free in all its parts and phases. Many socially relevant actions spring from passion, mental compulsion, uncritical imitation, habit, or from freedom. The proper approach might be suggested by the consideration that those phases of social behavior which can be described as the more profound, the more decisive, the more important (though not necessarily the more voluminous and conspicuous), the more formal, the more intelligible, and the more explanatory are also those in which freedom has the greater place. To exemplify the relation of the more formal to the less formal in human affairs, let us think of the daily discharge of our occupational duties. When it is time for me to go to the university I think of the papers that I shall need and I put them in my briefcase; I step into a bus, wait for a sign, get out of the bus, step into the elevator, push the button numbered 5, walk to the room numbered 509 and here I am, already busy opening letters. All these actions which involve but a little amount of free choice are contained in deeper actions marked by a higher degree of freedom. My daily behavior as a faculty member of the University of Chicago is contained within the free acts that I performed when, in answer to a most kind invitation, I decided to join the Committee on Social Thought. This was a free decision. It was not made impulsively out of passion or habit; it came at the end of a long deliberation. This free decision itself is contained in the most profound act of freedom elicited when I chose to be a philosopher rather than a business man or a musician. Notice, further, that the deep act of choosing one's vocation is itself contained in a deeper act of choice relative to the supreme ends of human life. Our decision to follow such and such a trade, whether honorable or not, was made on the basis of an anterior act of freedom by which we decided to live either a life of honesty or some other sort of life, to use our freedom according to the good or according to some other principle.[15]

Any socially relevant actions can be subjected to the same kind of analysis. It seems that in every case the processes clearly traceable to determinate causes take place on the material side of the picture, whereas the processes that play the part of forms originate in free choice. The genuine significance of the postulate of ethical neutrality is not epistemological; it is pedagogical. Inexperienced minds often embark upon social studies with a disorderly covetousness for judgments in terms of right and wrong. Such impatience and misdirected practical-mindedness jeopardize experimental investigations as well as rational analysis; these extremely harmful dispositions must be checked, by all means, from the outset. An attitude of ethical neutrality, understood in a purely pedagogical sense, may be a wise defense against the eagerness of practical minds not yet convinced that the true rules of action have to be sought with much patience through indirect procedures in which the purposes of action seem to be lost sight of.[16] The bad thing is that not a few professors fail to see the difference between a pedagogical indication and an objective necessity.

### From Social Science to the Philosophy of Society

Our schools are haunted by formulas and clichés which emphasize the independence and absoluteness of the fact. True, the fact is a sort of absolute, and primary importance attaches to the full recognition of its absoluteness. But a destructive illusion often creeps in at this point. We dream of safeguarding the "experimental attitude" by separating—if possible, completely—the statement of the fact from its interpretation. Yet, to state a fact is to assert that, beyond doubt, something exists, something happened, *some determinate object of thought* is or has been joined with the act of existing. The statement of a fact implies the apprehension—possibly very vague, possibly quite accurate—of some intelligible object. It implies the expression, the intelligible utterance, of this object in a concept of a certain type. If a fact belongs to the order of use—as distinct from the order of nature—its statement implies a minimum of interpretation in terms of the kind of plenitude, the kind of entirety, the kind of integrity that are proper to human use. But moral good is nothing else than this plenitude, and moral evil is nothing else than the corresponding privation. When the thing or event whose existence is asserted pertains to the order of use, the statement of fact normally contains some amount of interpretation in terms of right and wrong. Thus the postulate of ethical neutrality does not seem to hold even at the level of what is so confusedly called "purely empirical science" or "pure consideration of facts." In order to be entirely "pure" the consideration of facts would have to be devoid of intelligible expression. Science can be empiriological, that is, made of experiences animated by rational insights (*logoi*); but how could it be purely empirical? Empirical purity implies the elimination of the intelligible word (*logos*).

It is impossible to raise these issues without bringing in the problem of the relation between social science and the philosophy of society. Here also social thought was influenced by the example of physics. True, the relation between the scientific and the philosophic analyses of nature remains an exceedingly obscure issue. Apart from radical positivists who reject as "meaningless" all notion of a philosophy of nature, it is rather commonly held that there are two approaches to the physical world, one of which deserves to be called philosophical and the other does not. If we have definite ideas on the nature of philosophy, we may be able to elaborate on the meaning of this contrast. But even the best theorists know little about the relations between the scientific and the philosophic interpretations of nature. What they have to say, even if certainly sound, remains vague. Since human knowledge normally approaches perfection by moving from vagueness to precision, there is nothing shameful about being vague although it is a shame to do nothing about it. It is much worse to counterfeit precision when vagueness is the real state of affairs. As long as our directions are sound, a vague statement holds the promise of a precise one. Such promise may be contained in the consideration that the division of knowledge into science and philosophy seems to have less significance in the social order than in the physical order. This suggestion apparently follows from the law of interpretation which governs the apprehension of social experience. Facts pertaining to the life of human society seem to be of such character that a philosophy of man is necessarily at work in the reading of their intelligibility.

## NOTES

1. See F. A. Hayek, "Scientism and the Study of Society," *Economica*, 9 (1942), 267. At the beginning of this important essay, the

writer remarks that in the eighteenth and early nineteenth centuries "the study of economic and social phenomena was guided in the choice of its methods in the main by the nature of the problems it had to face." Yet the following footnote qualifies this statement: "This is, however, not universally true. The attempts to treat social phenomena 'scientifically,' which became so influential in the 19th century, were not completely absent in the 18th. There is at least a strong element of it in the work of Vico, of Montesquieu, and of the Physiocrats. But the great achievements of the century in the theory of the social sciences, the works of Cantillon and Hume, of Turgot and Adam Smith, were on the whole free from it."

2. Aristotle, *Politics* I, 11, 1259A7–22.

3. As an effect of oversimplification, the significance of this contrast has often been distorted. Alexandre Koyré rightly says that such a contrast, if not properly qualified, "ignores the technological effort of the Middle Ages." He remarks further that a certain "activistic" attitude, customarily ascribed to Renaissance physicists, is not so much that of Galileo or Descartes as that of Bacon "whose role, in the history of the scientific revolution, was altogether insignificant." *Etudes galiléennes.* I. *A L'Aube de la science classique* (Paris: Ecole Pratique des Hautes Etudes, 1939), p. 6.

4. Aristotle, *Metaphysics*, II, 2, 996B1; Thomas Aquinas, *Summa theol.* I, 5, 3 ad 4; Cajetan, commentary on this passage of the *Summa*; John of St. Thomas, *Curs. theol.* I, d. 6, a. 2, ed. Solesmes, I, 532ff.

5. In order that a being of reason be grounded in the real world, it does not suffice that its components be patterned after real entities, as is plain in the case of the chimera. Foundation in the real world implies a formal derivation, by reason of which some aspect of rational necessity passes over from the real world to the world of those entities which neither do nor can exist except in a purely objective capacity. A being of reason may result entirely from the synthetic power of imagination; in this case it has no law and admits of no definition, except insofar as a thing settled by convention can be defined. In the other case, the being of reason owes to its real origin a system of determinate features; consequently, it may be a scientific object second to none as far as rational necessity is concerned. Beings of reason with foundations in the real world are present in all sciences. They play a distinguished role in mathematics, whatever our definition of mathematics may be. They constitute the object of logic in its entirety.

6. The primary division of the sciences, in Aristotle, is tripartite, i.e., into theoretical, productive, and practical (*Metaphysics* VI, 1, 1025B19). Yet it is possible to vindicate an earlier division into theoret-

ical and practical sciences inasmuch as a science either is absolutely unconcerned with action (theoretical) or concerned with it either as a rule of production or as a rule of human action.

7. *On the Methodology of the Social Sciences*, trans. Edward A. Shils and Henry A. Finch (Glencoe, Ill.: Free Press, 1949).

8. Etienne Gilson, *Le Réalisme méthodique* (Paris: Tequi, 1936), p. 98. This remark does not by any means imply that the possibility and the necessity of a realistic notion of value should be questioned. For a realistic treatment of value, see Jacques Maritain, *Neuf Leçons sur les notions premières de la philosophie morale* (Paris: Tequi, 1951), and *Moral Philosophy: An Historical and Critical Survey of the Great Systems* (New York: Scribner's, 1964).

9. See *On the Methodology of the Social Sciences*, p. 22. Max Weber is very critical of the theory of trends.

10. An entirely realistic theory of values and of value-judgments is set forth in Maritain's *Neuf Leçons*. See, in particular, pp. 33, 38–66. The gist of this theory is forcefully expressed in the following sentences (p. 47): "Thus, moral values are a particular area, an area particular to human conduct, in the general domain of values antecedently acknowledged by the theoretical reason. If we consider things from this angle, we realize that the case of ethical values is not exceptional and that it belongs to an already known system, normal in all respects. Theoretical knowledge, metaphysics, philosophy of nature, the sciences of nature, medicine, logic overflow with value-judgments concerning the greater or lesser degree of a quality that should be there."

11. *Summa theol.* I–II, 94, 2. Quotations are from *Basic Writings of St. Thomas Aquinas*, ed. Anton Pegis (New York: Random House, 1945).

12. It is important to notice that Max Weber is less concerned with the question "Are value-judgments needed in order to understand social reality?" than with the question "Can social science demonstrate value-judgments and let us know what we have to do?" He answers both questions in the negative; yet it is clear that his main interest is to confute the theory, so popular in the nineteenth century, that a "positive" science should tell men what they ought to do in order to realize a rational and happy society.

13. This question is answered in the affirmative in a study that may well be the most thorough discussion of the postulate of ethical neutrality, *Natural Right and History* by Leo Strauss (Chicago: The University of Chicago Press, 1953), pp. 35–80.

At the beginning of his discussion, Strauss shows that social science, as a practical discipline concerned with means, must be guided by the knowledge of the ends and of the "Ought" if such knowledge is possible at all (p. 41). "Let us assume that we had genuine knowledge of right and wrong, or of the Ought, or of the true value system. That knowledge, while not derived from empirical science, would legitimately direct all empirical science; it would be the foundation of all empirical social science. For social science is meant to be of practical value. It tries to find means for given ends. For this purpose it has to understand the ends. Regardless of whether the ends are 'given' in a different manner from the means, the end and the means belong together; therefore, 'the end belongs to the same science as the means.' If there were genuine knowledge of the ends, that knowledge would naturally guide all search for means. There would be no reason to delegate knowledge of the ends of social philosophy and the search for the means to an independent social science. . . . The true reason why Weber insisted on the ethically neutral character of social science as well as of social philosophy was, then, not his belief in the fundamental opposition of the Is and Ought but his belief that there cannot be any genuine knowledge of the Ought. He denied to man any science, empirical or rational, any knowledge, scientific or philosophic, of the true value system: the true value system does not exist; there is a variety of values which are of the same rank, whose demands conflict with one another, and whose conflict cannot be solved by human reason. Social science or social philosophy can do no more than clarify that conflict and all its implications; the solution has to be left to the free, non-rational decision of each individual" (pp. 41–42).

Later, Strauss comes to what seems to me the essential point, viz., the theory that the interpretation of human facts in ethical terms pertains intrinsically to the understanding of these facts. "We remind ourselves again of Weber's statement about the prospects of Western civilization. As we observed, Weber saw the following alternative: either a spiritual renewal or else 'mechanized petrifaction,' i.e., the extinction of every human possibility except that of 'specialists without spirit or vision and voluptuaries without heart.' He concluded: 'But by making this statement we enter the province of judgments of value and faith with which this purely historical presentation shall not be burdened.' It is not proper, then, for the historian or social scientist, it is not permissible, that he truthfully describe a certain type of life as spiritually empty or describe specialists without vision and voluptuaries without heart as what they are. But is this not absurd? Is it not the plain duty of the social scientist truthfully and faithfully to present social phenomena? How can we give a causal explanation of a social phenomenon if we do not first see it as what it is? Do we not know petrifaction or spiritual emptiness when we see it? And if someone is incapable of seeing phenomena of this kind, is he not disqualified by this very fact from being a social scientist, just as much as a blind man is disqualified from being an analyst of painting" (pp. 49–50)?

14. Yves R. Simon, *Freedom of Choice*, ed. Peter Wolff (New York: Fordham University Press, 1969). See also Yves R. Simon, "Liberty and Authority," *Proceedings of the American Catholic Philosophical Association*, 16 (1940), 86–114.

15. To remove a possibility of misinterpretation, let it be said that the field in which freedom plays the most formal part obviously does not include the natural determinations which constitute the principle of freedom itself. The most profound act, in which even the choice of the last end (concretely considered) is contained, is the will to be happy, which is not free, but natural.

16. This pedagogical meaning of the principle of ethical neutrality is described by Weber in the following terms (*On the Methodology of the Social Sciences*, p. 5): "Today the student should obtain, from his teacher in the lecture hall, the capacity: (1) to fulfill a given task in a workmanlike fashion; (2) definitely to recognize facts, even those which may be personally uncomfortable, and to distinguish them from his own evaluations; (3) to subordinate himself to his task and to repress the impulse to exhibit his personal tastes or other sentiments unnecessarily."

# 5

# Christian Humanism: A Way to World Order

THE TITLE OF THIS CHAPTER can be interpreted both as a challenge and as an unreasonable promise. It suggests that Christian humanism is a thing great and powerful, whose beneficial effects are not restricted to any particular nation or culture. It also seems to convey wild ambitions. To be sure, we shall not set forth a program designed to bring about order in the world. The illusions that such a program would imply have been common in the context of social science, but anyone can see that they are out of place in the context of humanism. This contrast is striking and worth inquiring into.

### THE ILLUSIONS OF SOCIAL SCIENCE

When a trend of ideas has been going on for a considerable amount of time, it inevitably loses the sharpness of its primitive expressions, and its meaning, even if integrally preserved, is less certainly recognized. What gives the pre-Socratics unique significance in the history of philosophy is that they are too primitive to bother about the conventions of good academic society; they express things such as they see them, with no fears and no tactical subtleties. In the earliest phase of the nineteenth century, Henri Saint-Simon stands like a pre-Socratic character, fearless and uninhibited. The ideal of a science designed to render society rational and happy is expressed in his work with the lucidity of youthful enthusiasm. Students of contemporary ideologies know that this ideal never died out. But by reason of their forceful frankness Saint-Simon and his disciples remain our best source on science as a factor of world order.

The school of Saint-Simon emphasizes the influence that the science of nature exercises upon society by proposing new and better goals to human energies. For them, the exploitation of man has been at all times the purpose of government. But as an effect of scientific enlightenment men are developing a novel interest in the industrial transformation of physical nature; correspondingly, they lose interest in the exploitation of their fellow men. The government of persons disappears into an administration of things. Saint-Simon was not a liberal, and his followers were possessed of a strongly authoritarian spirit; yet the anarchistic philosophy of the nineteenth century derived from them the theory that in the industrial age the state is bound to wither away.

Inasmuch as science is applied to society itself, leadership loses the character of authority and becomes the privilege of impersonal expertness. Because of ignorance we are divided with regard to ways and means; our action is hopelessly crippled by disunity unless some men are empowered to make decisions binding for all. But social science, by demonstrating what ways lead to what ends, renders authority superfluous. The sovereignty of the people becomes as absurd and subversive as that of the traditional king. Science alone is sovereign. The lawmakers have been displaced by the interpreters of social nature.

The scientific reorganization of society will procure peace. At all times war has been waged in order to establish or maintain the domination of man over man. By promoting industry, science discourages domination and fosters association. In the words of Saint-Simon, soon used as a motto by his followers, the golden age, which was placed by the poets' imagination at the origin of the human species, "in the ignorance and the crudeness of the first times," actually lies before us, in the universal brotherhood of men associated for the exploitation of the earth.

From the standpoint of the present inquiry, the relevant characteristics of this philosophy are three. First, it disregards contingency. To be sure, contingent occurrences cannot be treated scientifically. If we hold that society should be ruled by scientific judgment, we also hold that there is no room for contingency in social affairs—a very arbitrary assumption. Second, inasmuch as patterns derived from physical science and techniques are held capable of bringing about the perfection of human order, it is assumed that the causes at work in social life belong to the same system as those at work in physical nature—another arbitrary assumption, by which the role of free choice is ignored. Third, this philosophy is marked by the extreme optimism of the eighteenth century. Provided truth is established scientifically, promulgated by teaching, and corroborated by the emotional power of preaching, there will be little or no resistance. It seems that coercion will soon become unnecessary.

These illusions have been badly shaken by the great catastrophes of the twentieth century. We no longer believe that men trained in the sciences, techniques, and industrial crafts are thereby disinclined to lust for domination over their fellow men. In our worried inquiries into culture and education we listen with some eagerness to the suggestion that after all the so-called humane studies may have a unique way of tending to make men more human. At this point, some informal remarks on the notion of humanism will be more helpful than a formal definition. Let it be said that humanism can be understood both as an attitude and as a culture. (Shifting appropriately from humanism as attitude to humanism as culture and vice-versa will be one of the difficulties of this exposition.) As an attitude it is characterized by respect for *all* men and confidence in the ability of mankind to accomplish good things in *this* world. It is not necessarily optimistic, but it is necessarily confident. And if a friend of man expects great things of his fellow men, but only in the other world, he cannot be described as a humanist.

With regard to humanism as a culture, a few historical references make up an adequate substitute for a definition. We know very well what we mean when we set in opposition the Scholastics and the Humanists of the time of Erasmus or when we say that the French writers of the seventeenth century had a strong background of humanistic education. Again, if I say that a certain professor is a good humanist but by no means a philosopher, everyone will understand me perfectly.

Far from believing that science and technique will ever be by themselves a cause of order and wisdom in the world, we have come to suspect that a technical culture may involve definite threats to the attitudes that foster the understanding of man, cooperation, and brotherhood. Let us consider, first, an intellectual bias that persons dedicated to scientific work can hardly avoid. Inasmuch as theoretical science strives toward explanation, it proceeds by way of analysis, which is the same as saying that it traces effects to their essential causes and consequences to their essential principles. Now, in most cases, analysis involves the decomposition of a whole into its parts; this is not strictly necessary, and it is easy to think of cases in which analysis traces effects to the whole and brings forth the power of the whole. But to produce a bias it suffices that a procedure should occur with great frequency. In fact, the consideration of the parts fills most of the time given to scientific analysis. The result is that a mind trained in theoretical disciplines is not particularly well prepared to understand, in things and in persons, the problems pertaining to the whole as such. These remarks apply to philosophy as well as to the other sciences.

Even within his own field, the theorist is ill at ease when the effects to be explained call for an analysis into the powers of the whole. The misadventure told by Mephistopheles[1] is common among biologists and philosophers of life. The case is much worse when the analyst has to deal with practical issues. Men trained in theoretical disciplines are often poor psychologists, in the ordinary and practical sense of the word psychology. They may be very good at measuring sense perception, at defining the effects of diverse chemicals on emotions, or at explaining how free choice proceeds from rational knowledge. No one should question the value of these analyses. But when such people are thrown into the world of action, say, as citizens or statesmen, they are likely to evidence inadequate preparation. True, what matters in the handling of men is not so much what we know about the laws of sense perception, memory, intelligence, and will as our ability to understand men as wholes and persons. We have just recalled the contrast between the Scholastics and the Humanists of the sixteenth century. These Scholastics do not entirely deserve their bad reputation. Not all were bad and some were very great. But inasmuch as the movement of civilization demanded new insights into man considered as a whole, into man considered holistically and historically as a free agent engaged in an irreversible adventure, the Scholastics had little to offer. Even the greatest of them, St. Thomas, sometimes gives poor answers to questions involving psychological accidents. St. Augustine is better acquainted with such questions, which accounts, in part, for the readiness of many Humanists to accept Augustinian directions.

In a spirit of devotion to St. Thomas Aquinas, some of our colleges are today essaying programs which lay special emphasis on philosophy and theology. Roughly, it can be said that in these programs philosophy and theology, rather than the humanities, constitute the substance of liberal education. A philosopher cannot help rejoicing whenever philosophy is honored, and if he is a Christian he has stronger reasons to value any action designed to increase the influence of theology. As it generally happens with programs, these are objectionable not by reason of what they include but by reason of what they may exclude. Suppose that the amount of time given to philosophy and theology makes it impossible to achieve any thoroughness in humanistic studies: the program might not be conducive to the understanding of men under the conditions of totality which are decisively significant in all social relations. A philosopher must grant that, when there is need for an holistic approach to human realities, philosophy has no further claim on the student's time.

Let us now consider a psychological problem relative to the physical power born of scientific knowledge. Familiarity with the accomplishments of technique fills the minds of men with patterns of irresistible efficiency and faultless regularity. In contrast with these images of order, man is the only thing that causes disorder with appalling frequency. Not so long ago most machines were subject to frequent accidents, but in the last few years the mechanical environment of mankind has been speaking, with ever increased firmness, the language of predictability, regularity, faithfulness, order. Contradiction came from man.

In our speculations about social becoming we are used to treating the natural and the technical environments as systems of material causes whose transformations increase or restrict the possibilities open to human initiative. We feel that we have done our duty if we have carefully measured the part played by such formal causes as ideas, faiths, and opinions, and the part played by such material causes as soil and tools. Yet we are all familiar with a development in which the technical environment, over and above all it does in the order of material causality, plays with striking efficacy the role of exemplary cause. I am referring to belief in progress. Throughout the eighteenth and nineteenth centuries, commonly received ideas about human progress involved illusions of such magnitude that it is not easy to see how they could be received by sane persons. Do not overrate the power of vicious propagandists interested in spreading the rumor that the problem of evil was just about to be solved. Rather, consider that until the First World War nothing could hold in check the influence of the pattern set by continual progress in the technical environment of daily life. Today, the trend of our techniques keeps speaking of progress, but it also speaks, with unprecedented persuasiveness, of order, and men are just as disorderly as they have ever been. Hence a new kind of resentment, which arouses each of us against his fellow men and divides each from the other. Sometimes we no longer understand why our beloved ones behave as they do instead of following the good example set for them by machines which do so faithfully what they are supposed to do. Much of the difference between the contemporary totalitarian state and the tyrannies of the past can be traced to the new patterns of regularity. We feel that there is in mankind something that ought to be crushed. A highly developed technical environment has given birth to a particularly frightful kind of misanthropy.

The age of the Renaissance, which produced unprecedentedly important developments in humanistic culture, also produced the modern interpretation of nature. In relation to the problems of humanism, the most significant feature of the physical system founded by Galileo and Descartes is that it ignores finality. From now on man will be alone among the things of this world. He is a creature with tendencies, desires, purposes, and meaningful activities. Physical things will no longer be companions to him. The surrounding world is no longer a universe of natures: it is made of only one entity—call it extension or space—and this entity is not a nature.

Opposition to finalistic interpretations proceeds from a variety of factors, some of which are altogether incidental and boil down to misunderstandings. It happens, for instance, that a biologist makes vehement utterances against finality because he has felt the danger of unwarranted explanations by final causes and does not possess the instruments needed to distinguish between the relevant and the meaningless problems of finality. But, considered in its basic trends, the physical science born of the Renaissance ignores finality for a reason that pertains to its essential constitution. This science is a mathematical reading of the physical world. As far as its form is concerned, it is mathematical, and consequently foreign to the study of final causes. The remnants of teleological explanation that are found in modern science evidence a resistance on the part of the physical content and a failure of the mathematical form to assert its proper effects. The exclusion of finalistic notions results from the nature of mathematical abstraction. Objects treated mathematically have lost the relation to existence that desirability implies. As Aristotle says, there is no goodness in mathematical entities. Mathematical sciences are good, but mathematical objects are not. You may fall in love with mathematics—many people do—but you cannot fall in love with the square root of minus one.

It is by no means obvious that the mathematical interpretation of nature, with its success, rules out any other scientific approach to the physical world. If a philosophy of nature of the Aristotelian type, a philosophical physics, had maintained its position at the time of the Renaissance and had demonstrated its ability to achieve progress under the new circumstances, the cultural meaning of natural science might have been widely different from what it has come to be. In fact, the philosophy of nature has been displaced by modern physics. As a result of bewildering success in the mathematical interpretation of nature, the universe of culture was split. In sharp contrast with the physical world, which is described as foreign to finality and to intelligent order, the human world remains characterized by tendencies, aspirations, and manifest destinies such as the defeat of ignorance, less suffering, a longer life, peaceful cooperation among men. As long as belief in natural law and in the metaphysical worth of man was strong, the vision of human affairs remained finalistic. But the threat of a violent reduction to unity appears as soon as the minds yield to the fascination of a social science which, in order to deal with mankind as successfully as physics does with nature, has to take on the scientific features of physics and to dismiss "unscientific prejudices," the most flagrant of which is explanation by final causes. In contemporary atheism, the non-finalistic pattern is applied, regardless of the cost, to the totality of human affairs. Not only physical nature, but also mankind and its history have become a tale told by an idiot, signifying nothing. An all-embracing picture of absurdity expresses the last word of a mechanistic philosophy which has grown into a violent negation of all that humanism values. In some respects existentialism is an effort to achieve decency in a world whose meaninglessness extends to human actions.

## The Conflict Between Humanism and Christianity

At a time when absurdity enjoys such prominence at the vanguard of philosophy, ethics, and literature, it seems that a program of Christian humanism should have a significant part to play in the struggle for the conservation and progress of many things precious to man. Yet the very notion of Christian humanism raises difficulties, for the relations of humanism and religion have often been marked by conflicts. It is of decisive importance that the meaning of these conflicts be ascertained.

Remarkably, several of the processes that make up the development of modern humanism coincided with periods of intense concern for the theological issues of grace, nature, and fall. The dogma of original sin suggests a dark picture of the human condition: it may be so interpreted as to exclude the attitude of confidence that humanism implies. In Jansenism and in some sections of Protestantism, received theories on the state of man after the fall are hardly compatible with humanistic ideals.

Pascal is the greatest of the Jansenists, though by no means the most Jansenistic of them; he is a mathematician and a physicist whose representation of the world is not free from mechanistic influences; he is an *honnête homme*, deeply trained in the humanities and a reader of Montaigne. He is also a moralist who distrusts man. Ultimately he is too much of a Jansenist to be a humanist. Irving Babbitt writes that "when an austere Christian, such as Pascal, considers man in his fallen estate . . . he quickly arrives at conclusions regarding the secular order and its political problems that are, if possible, more Machiavellian than those of Machiavelli himself."[2] The paradoxes of Pascal on law and justice involve theological issues that pertain directly to the theory of Christian humanism. St. Thomas Aquinas has worked out to perfection all the philosophic instruments needed for the treatment of these issues, but these instruments are unfamiliar to Pascal.

In the doctrine of Aquinas the state of original innocence is defined by two systems of gifts, supernatural and preternatural. The supernatural gifts of innocence enabled man to know and love God on a level of excellence that no created or creatable thing can attain by its own power. The preternatural gifts protected him from hardships to which he is naturally subject. Original sin caused the loss of all superadded perfections. Now, these could not be removed without nature itself being wounded. Thus, the consequences of original sin are of two kinds, formal and material. Its formal consequences are the wounds of nature, the disquieting propensities and the incapacities that would not have existed if man had been created in the state of pure nature. Its material consequences are natural conditions that were preternaturally suspended by the gifts of innocence; of these conditions original sin is cause in a merely historical sense. It is natural for man to die, to be subject to disease, to irksome labor, to error, and to precariousness in the possession of truth and virtue.

Not enough attention has been given to Pascal's extremely optimistic notion of human nature considered apart from its wounds. Maritain wrote that where Pascal says with indignation "corrupted nature," St. Thomas often says, with compassion, "human nature." The inordinate judgments of Pascal on the corruption of nature are connected with an inordinate appraisal of man's natural possibilities. The contrast between his exalted idea of uncorrupted nature and his experience of human reality accounts to a large extent for the bitterness of his expressions about natural law and political justice. "There are doubtless natural laws, but that fine corrupted reason of ours has corrupted everything. . . . Strange justice that is limited by a river! Truth on this side of the Pyrenees, error on the other side."[3] "Justice is subject to controversy, but might is recognized easily and without any controversy. It has not been possible to render justice mighty, because might contradicted justice and said that itself (might) was just. And thus, because it proved impossible to give might to justice, men have decided that might was just."[4] "He who obeys laws because they are just, obeys a justice of his imagination, not the essence of the law; law is altogether self-contained; it is law and nothing more."[5] With a mind free from the optimistic visions which haunt the background of Pascal's anthropology it is easy to see that justice is not totally absent from temporal history, in spite of the wounds of sin. Struggle for justice is not doomed to failure. It is not altogether impossible to cause what is just to be strong; it is only very difficult. To be sure, we cannot establish a perfect and unshakable justice, but it is up to us to multiply the victories of an imperfect and precarious justice which is worth our dying for it.

In our time, all issues involving optimism or pessimism, confidence or hopelessness, are marked by the consequences of the great waves of disappointment which unfurled on the Western World in 1914 and in the years following the First World War. Atrocious experiences terminated abruptly a century and a half of optimistic expectations. The affective situation brought about by the First World War and the following crises comprises a frightful array of destructive passions: lust for military glory, admiration of force, desire to crush, to exterminate, to annihilate, hatred aimed at groups, scorn for personal innocence, and eagerness to substitute the pleasures of collective intoxication for the dignity of truth and freedom. We are tempted to say that catastrophic occurrences have opened a new era of pessimism, but the psychology to which we are referring is better described in terms of disappointed optimism. It has been remarked in the foregoing that humanism is necessarily confident, though not necessarily optimistic. True, there is such a thing as confident pessimism. A soul firmly established in a fearless knowledge of evil may be possessed of serene energy. All that moral pessimism (as opposed to metaphysical pessimism) implies is a deep realization of our wretchedness, an uninhibited disposition to see evil wherever it appears and wherever it is hidden, and a keen vision of the difficulties that must be overcome if any genuine good is to be achieved. In some minds pessimistic propositions express nothing else than the profundity of moral intelligence. There is no reason why such profundity should ever cause hopelessness and resentment. A pessimist may be a humanist. But disappointed optimists are generally inclined to misanthropic attitudes. Before disappointment came, they used to bear in mind unwarranted claims and expectations. Experience has not corrected their frame of mind. They remain convinced that things should not be so difficult as they actually are, and that something has gone wrong as an effect of unforgivable viciousness, by the deliberate will of bad people who must be punished, even though it may be too late to restore the harmony that they have destroyed.

Christian society did not prove immune to the dark passions born of disappointed optimism, and whereas these passions often resulted in the persecution of Christians, we have witnessed, among persons of the same faith, the growth of a distinctly pious misanthropy. Of all the moral trends that have shaped the world of our time, this one is the least advertised, though by no means the least significant. Things inconspicuous may be active at a very deep level, and, by reason of depth, achieve far-reaching influence in spite of their small volume.

In the psychological complex that we are attempting to describe, the disappointments of the twentieth century assume a particular meaning. There is, in the background, a tradition firmly opposed to common illusions on necessary progress, both in regard to form and in regard to content: in regard to form, because Christians know that mankind is not necessitated to make the right choices; in regard to content, because they know that many things commonly exalted as facts of progress are errors, mistakes, misfortunes of utmost gravity. Thus, when the great catastrophes came, some Christians were tempted to find a sarcastic pleasure in the realization that a dismal interpretation of human nature had been forced upon men; not all of them resisted this temptation with complete success. But as soon as there is the slightest touch of sarcasm in the relation of a Christian to his fellow men, all sentiments, the loftiest included, are affected by deadly falsity. Under the cover of uncompromising zeal for truth and morality, a never-ending set of negations is evoked. Any reform that embodies a hope is scoffed at. The only welcome reforms are those that confirm a failure and the frustration of a hope. Support is systematically given to government by the few, though the basic assumptions are not the same as in the conventional philosophy of aristocratic government. The theory of aristocracy demands that the few in charge of government be the best. For the negativists with whom we have to do, expecting the political leaders to escape the general wretchedness would be another case of despicable naïveté, and when these leaders happen to be, as in some famous contemporary instances, the very worst of criminals, some enjoyment can still be found in the feeling that once more hope has been frustrated. The core of the system is made of a certain attitude toward man as a sinner. It is something subtle, secret, tragic, and dreadfully simple. Indeed, for any religious soul, the greatest cause of indignation is the way in which God is treated by men. But, by a deviation that takes place in the darkness of confused conscience, the indignation aroused by man's ungratefulness to God sometimes grows into resentment, desire to punish, aversion, rejection. A sentiment originating in faith and love has been corrupted into an aggressive form of melancholy.

## Humanism and Christianity: A Possible Synthesis

We have described two cases in which the connection between unhumanistic attitude and religion is entirely accidental, and traceable to a deficient operation of the religious virtues or of their instruments. In the case of the seventeenth-century Jansenist, the rational instruments at the service of faith—i.e., the theories concerning nature, goodness, freedom, sin, etc.—are not pure and strong enough to show under what conditions humanism is compatible with Christian dogma. In the case of the contemporary negativist, the deficiency seems to be almost entirely comprised within the secret sphere of religious and moral sentiments. Let us now ask whether it is possible to say, in general terms, that any conflict between humanism and Christian religion is accidental and can be traced to some deficiency, either on the part of the humanist or on the part of the religious man. To be sure, no necessary feature of humanism is incompatible with any feature essential to Christianity. Yet the proposition that conflicts between humanism and Christianity are always accidental will be misleading unless it is supplemented by the understanding of tendencies which, without being essential, are factually permanent and will never be disposed of.

Christian beliefs concerning original sin do not exclude the confident vision of man that humanism implies, but they contain a warning against the myths of naturalistic optimism. The Christian knows how easily the confidence of the humanist deteriorates into a rejection of the supernatural order. Correspondingly the humanist is permanently tempted to see in Christian mysteries a threat to his exalted notion of man. The solution lies in a humanistic theory that places at the center of its universe the union of divine and human natures in Christ. But we cannot expect a thing as precious as the *humanism of the Incarnation* (Maritain) to enjoy a peaceful existence and an harmonious development, free from ruptures of equilibrium. The relations of humanism and Christianity will always involve risks and be subject to phases of conflict. Such a condition would be sufficiently accounted for by the psychological contexts in which Christian doctrine and humanistic ideas are engaged. But the case is made more serious by the weight of an enormous historical accident.

Modern humanism was brought into existence by a wave of admiration for the literary masterpieces of Greece and Rome. Down to our time humanistic culture has comprised, as its most fundamental component, a loving acquaintance with monuments of pagan sensibility, pagan ethics, pagan views on life and death, pagan wisdom. True, the ideal of a Christian humanism was familiar to some of the earliest humanists. Throughout the classical age intensive studies of Greek and Latin literature were conducted within programs of Christian education distinguished by their generous and conquering spirit. Not a few humanists had the privilege of living close to saintly influences and some humanists were saints. The system of Christian education which prevailed in the classical age is responsible for much greatness and much beauty, and no one would question that it played an important part in the development of Christian culture. Remarkably, some of its shortcomings seem to be traceable to the inordinate power of un-Christian models. In the Christian society of the seventeenth century, trends that matter decisively for the shaping of mores and civilization escape, to a large extent, the influence of Christianity. Consider, for instance, the sense of honor which contributes so much to the glory of this period. It is a sentiment of great ethical and social value; in an appropriate system of subordinations it might be the instrument of the loftiest Christian virtues. But such as it exists in the fearless society of the seventeenth century, the sense of honor is so foreign to Christianity that it often leads men to face death in glorious actions described as criminal by Christian ethics. The Cid, a dramatic character who belongs both to Spain and to France, embodies admirably the chivalrous ideal of the time. According to Christian belief, a judgment does follow the death to which he exposes himself so bravely for the defense of his honor. In this perspective the character of the Cid becomes absurd. To enjoy the tragedy the spectator must forget what he knows about the Christian meaning of life and death. Apparently such abstraction was easily effected by sincere Christians brought up, at school, amid tales of pagan fortitude.

The connection between classical humanism and pagan antiquity must be borne in mind when there is a question of understanding the transition from the humanism of the sixteenth and seventeenth centuries to the humanism of later generations. The former is generally intended to be Christian; at least it is not intended to be un-Christian. But in the eighteenth and nineteenth centuries humanism takes on a definitely naturalistic character. It often expresses a claim for freedom from revelation and identifies itself with free thought, secularism, agnosticism, and finally atheism. In this movement away from Christianity it remains close to the pagan models traditionally proposed, ever since the Renaissance, to the admiration of the youth: recall the worship of the Plutarchian heroes in the French Revolution. For the philosophers of religion, humanism comes to designate a theory which interprets divine attributes as mythical magnifications of human traits and for which all the religious past of mankind proclaims the supremacy of man.

The tendencies which so often set humanism in opposition to Christianity will never die out: at best we can expect a situation in which it will not be too difficult to keep them under control. We would like to know whether we actually find ourselves in such a situation. An answer in the affirmative is suggested by the evolution of ideas on natural law. In the eighteenth century and in the earlier part of the nineteenth century the philosophy of natural law was often associated with an aversion to revealed truth, with free thought and a proud assertion of human independence. But today belief in natural law has become uncommon in circles foreign to religion; where it is strong it is generally associated with faith in revelation and grace. The condition of the human understanding is such that our knowledge of natural truth, with regard to subjects that concern our destiny in the most direct fashion, is badly deficient and precarious whenever the power of natural reason is not strengthened by the obscure certainties of faith. Natural reason can attain many truths concerning God, but this rational ability is so subject to accident that the metaphysics of God seems bound to quick decadence as soon as faith is no longer there to direct the work of the reason. (It is hardly necessary to recall that these considerations are entirely relative to the *state*, i.e., the existential condition of metaphysical truths in the human mind, and do not concern the intrinsic laws of these truths and the way in which they must be established in order to pertain to metaphysical science.) What holds for the best and most difficult parts of metaphysics also holds for ethics. The theory of natural law is by definition something entirely natural and entirely rational. If our reason were in a perfect state of health, we should be able not only to perceive as absolutely obvious the axioms of natural law but also to establish with full clarity any particular proposition deductively connected with these axioms. But experience reveals a discrepancy between a *de jure* possibility and what is possible *de facto*. The circumstances of our time make it clear that the knowledge of natural law is firmest and most lucid when it is associated with faith in God as cause of the supernatural order. Far from being tempted to use natural law as an argument against the divine government of mankind, we are aware that the theory of natural law, which is the foundation of all consistent humanism, finds its best guarantee within Christian faith. We have learned to seek in the supernatural order the accomplishment of man's autonomy. Precisely because these dispositions have been acquired at a very high cost, through the wasteland of atheism and absurdity, they are likely to endure. They may characterize a period of cultural development. Just at the time when the impact of science and technique on human affairs urgently suggests a renewal of humane culture, the religious situation seems to provide adequate guarantees against the risks that a humanistic attitude and a humanistic culture inevitably involve. Let us also remark that a program of humanism in education worked out in our time could include a much larger amount of Christian substance than any program conceived in the sixteenth or seventeenth century. Many great works of Christian genius posterior to the Renaissance have, by now, sufficiently aged in the memory of mankind to satisfy the historical requirements of the humanistic approach. Moreover, we have come to appreciate the Middle Ages, which the men of the Renaissance ignored or despised. There is no longer any reason why pagan models should fill the mind of the Christian humanist.

It is easy to see by what features a humanistic education is able to counteract the disquieting tendencies brought about by familiar acquaintance with scientific objects and technical creations. The humanistic approach to man is holistic. Think, for instance, of the knowledge of man achieved through the study of the Greek tragedies, the plays of Shakespeare, the Spanish theater, and the French dramatists of the seventeenth century. Many writers of drama are famous for their penetrating analyses. But the power of dramatic life constantly asserts the unity of the human character and forestalls any tendency toward an analytical disintegration of the type described by Mephistopheles. The spiritual link of totality and personality is always present. It is grasped intuitively. Even though the course of events be dominated by tragic inevitability, human freedom, whether defeated or not, stands at the center of the work. Nothing is less dramatic than a utopian fiction in which beings falsely called human exhibit the kind of reliability that we like to find in machines. A society ideally responsive to propaganda would be unable to produce a dramatic situation, and, conversely, familiar association with dramatic heroes is a sound way to exclude the ruthless utopia of a society shaped by technological patterns of order.

Inasmuch as humanism is expected to remedy a situation brought about by science and technique, it is inevitable that the humanistic and the technical cultures be set in opposition to each other. Whether such opposition should be emphasized, made systematic and dominant is a question of great practical significance. In many cases the defenders of humanistic culture are people who hate our technological society. They are ill-adjusted to the mechanical environment, they curse it, and they extend the curse to the sciences of which techniques are so many applications. The least that can be said of such opposition is that it involves a waste of time, for there is not the slightest chance that mankind will give up its technological conquests. Striving to preserve, in an increasingly technological society, islands of simple life where man may resume communication with untamed nature would be an altogether different proposition, reasonable, and free from the crippling effects of a hopeless conflict with historical reality. Let it be pointed out that an harmonious relation to the course of history is essential to humanism. An unhistorical humanism, a humanism with no understanding for what is going on in this world, is necessarily ungenuine, for humanism is not an abstract science of human nature: it is a sympathetic approach to what history has made of man.

In the broad organism of the sciences and the techniques, some functions regard the contemplation of truth and pertain to contemplative life: these functions are above the space where humanism is expected to exercise its ordering power; let them be left apart, and let us call "technical culture" the whole set of the functions that are either technical by nature or preparatory to technique. The fruitful task is to establish, between the technical and the humanistic cultures, a relation of instrument to principal cause, the kind of relation exemplified by the brush and the painter. There is nothing, in a wonderful painting, that has not been really caused by the brush acting in the capacity of instrument. Any thing used in the instrumental capacity is capable of bringing about effects with no definite proportion to its own nature, as the tool of the artist causes, among other things, the spiritual splendor of the work of art. Our problem is to make it sure that the technical acts as an instrument at the service of the human. One way to contribute to this desirable state of affairs is to place technical culture in instrumental subordination to humanistic culture. Let us consider one example.

In our discussion of academic programs we sometimes ask whether the sciences should be taught in an extratemporal condition or in the context of their own history. I know scientists who blame me bitterly when they catch me reading a scientific book written forty years ago. For them, teaching science is teaching the latest expression of scientific progress; for them, anything that falls short of the last word of science serves only to slow down the development of the science student. Such a stand, no doubt, is borne out by very strong considerations. Another method has been popularized by the Great Books movement. In some colleges the *Elements* of Euclid and the *Principles* of Newton are given a place similar to that of Plato's *Timaeus* and Descartes' *Meditations*. True, we used to set in contrast the tendency of scientific works to disappear into the past of science and the aptitude of philosophic works to endure as part of philosophy's everlasting present. Everyone, in our time, knows that Euclid's geometry is insufficiently formalized and that the physics of Newton is objectionable in several aspects. To some extent the *Elements* and the *Principles* belong to the past of science, but, no less than the dialogues of Plato and the treatises of Descartes, they belong to the history of the human mind and to the history of our societies: over and above what they have to say on figures and movements, these great scientific works express the relation of science to human effort, to human failure, to human adventure. Such considerations may not refute the theory that, on certain levels of teaching at least, nothing outweighs the duty of giving the student the most finished product of science. I do not wish to declare myself in favor of either position. I wish only to remark that, whatever its faults may be, the reading of Euclid and Newton has the advantage of favoring the instrumental subordination of the technical to the human.

In every relation of instrumentality a special problem may result from the weight of the instrument. A good instrument is one that is obediently traversed by the power of the principal agent. If there is a question of repairing a watch, a heavy tool can easily defeat the skill of the craftsman. The difficulties caused by the weight of the instrument are frightful in the case of the techniques that we have created to make ourselves masters and possessors of physical nature. Man is often dragged, by the sheer heaviness of his techniques, where he does not want to go. Can any general principle direct our effort to resolve, in every particular case, the conflict between the weight of our instruments and the law of instrumentality? The spirit of poverty supplies the answer. In the relation of the human to the technical, we keep our instruments under control insofar as we remain free from attachment to things inferior to man. But it is not only in our relation to the physical world that we have to overcome the weight of things instrumental. Within all the system of our intellectual culture, what should be obedient often is heavy, and the freedom of the higher energies never can be taken for granted; again it is the spirit of poverty, the spirit of freedom from attachment to things inferior, that preserves the order of human salvation and removes the danger of man's being crushed by the weight of his ideas, his systems, his experiences, his erudition, his constructs, his methods, and his postulations. The quest for freedom from whatever is heavy, within the mind as well as in man's dealing with nature and the works of his own art, thus leads us to consider the relation of humanism to what is above it. A program of humanistic studies should not exclude the masterpieces of mystical literature. Clearly, mysticism, which is totally concerned with eternal life, does not in any sense pertain to such an essentially human and historical thing as humanistic culture. But an inspiration derived from mystical life, and ultimately from the sovereign simplicity of mystical contemplation, is precisely what humanism needs in order to be vitally Christian and to ensure, in all domains and on all levels, the freedom of man from the weight of man's creations.

## NOTES

1. Goethe, *Faust*, Part I, lines 1936–39. See above, chap. 1, p. 5–6.
2. *Democracy and Leadership* (Boston and New York: Houghton Mifflin, 1924), p. 37.
3. *Pensées*, ed. Léon Brunschvicg (Paris: Hachette, 1971), no. 294.
4. Ibid., no. 298.
5. Ibid., no. 294.

# INDEX

Affective knowledge
  and the common good, 26
  and inclination, 18ff.
  and incommunicability, 24
  *see also* Connaturality
Analysis and synthesis
  and literature, 152
  and synthesis of realization, 52
  and theoretical science, 52, 57
  Methods of, 8–9, 102, 140
  *see also* Command
Aquinas, St. Thomas, vii, xii, 110, 141
  and Christian humanism, 145
  and contemplation, 80, 82
  and science, 101
  and studiosity and curiosity, 66ff.
  and virtue, 56–57
  Fact and value in, 124
Aristotle, vii, xii, 66, 91, 113, 143
  and definition of virtue, 56–57
  and division of intellectual virtues, 41
  and division of sciences, 120
  and moral science, 43ff., 45, 112–13
  and operations of the mind, 62
  and psychology, 47, 128
  and science, x, 85
  and social science, 120
Art, 10, 28
  and practical wisdom, 50
Asceticism, 93
Augustine, St., 120, 141
  and definition of virtue, 10, 56–57
  and understanding of Socrates, 112–13
Authority, 26

Babbitt, Irving, 81, 145
Bacon, Francis, 116

Balzac, Honoré de, 87, 104
Baudelaire, Charles, 87, 104
Bergson, Henri, 6, 38n6
Berlin, Isaiah, 38n5
Blondel, Maurice, 6
Boutroux, Emile
   His understanding of Socrates, 43, 113
Bréhier, Emile
   on Christian philosophy, 88

Calvinism, 22
Certainty
   and moral philosophy, 70, 102
   of practically practical knowledge, 111
   of prudential judgments, 70, 102
   of truth, 11
Christian ethics
   contrasted with natural ethics, 66, 90
Command, viii, ix, 3
   and explanation, 27
   and formal causality, ix, 5, 20
   and incommunicability, 71
   and intelligibility, 79
   and the synthesis of realization, 8, 52
   and the ultimate practical judgment, 4, 17, 108, 111
   and use, 10
Communicability
   and demonstration, 24
   of science and philosophy, 117
Condorcet, Marquis de, 39n16
Connaturality, 20
   and knowledge of contingents, 35
   and natural law, 33
   and practically practical knowledge, 104, 107
   *see also* Affective knowledge

Descartes, René, 48, 62, 154
   and demiurgical ambitions of science, 116
   and mystery, 34
   and non-teleological physics, 142
   Dualism of, 122
   Method of, 24

[Ps.-]Dionysius, 55
Divorce, 94
Dostoevski, Feodor, 87, 104

Einstein, Albert, 73
Empiriological, 49
  contrasted with empirical, 77*n*9, 132
Epicureans, 120
Erasmus, Desiderius, 139
Euclid, 154
Existentialism, 144
Explanation
  and fulfillment, ix, 75, 97, 100, 105–106, 112
  Distinguished from theoretical explanation, 84
  Historical need for, x, 74, 97
  Practical, 83, 102, 109

Finality
  and modern science, 117, 122, 142
  and nature, xi, 68
Free will
  and superdeterminate causality, 129

Galileo, 72, 143
Gilson, Etienne, 122
  and Christian philosophy, 88
Great Books, The, 154

Hayek, F. A., 132*n*1
History
  and progress, 123
  and scientific explanation, 101, 108, 112
Humanism
  characterized, 139
  and Christianity, xi, 149, 152, 133
  Modern, 144, 149
Hume, David, 63–64

Ignorance, 14
*The Imitation of Christ*, 56
*Imperium*
  *see* Command

Inclination
  Knowledge by, 32, 97
  *see also* Connaturality

James, William, 6, 48
Jansenism, 22
  and humanism, 144
John of the Cross, St., 80, 82
  and practically practical knowledge, 86, 101–102
John of St. Thomas, St.
  and knowledge by inclination, 17
  and moral philosophy, 32, 58–60, 101
  and practical science, 109–11

Kant, Immanuel, 22, 63–65, 122
Koyré, Alexandre, 133*n*3

Leibniz, Gottfried Wilhelm von, 48
Liberal education, 141
Lucretius, 48

Machiavelli, Niccolò, 145
Mandonnet, Pierce
  and Christian philosophy, 88
Maritain, Jacques, vii, viii, 61, 134*n*10, 145
  and Christian humanism, 149
  and Christian philosophy, 89
  and moral philosophy adequately taken, 95
  and practically practical knowledge, 80–87
Meredith, George, 87, 104
Meyerson, Emile, 83–84
Mill, John Stuart, 48
Montaigne, Michel Eyquem de, 145
  as moralist, 81, 87, 104, 108
Moral philosophy, x, 28
  adequately taken, 95, 98, 105
  and explanation, 106
  and practical wisdom, 53ff., 59, 102
  and theoretically practical science, 55
  and truth, 55, 68
  and use, 60
Moral science, x, 22, 28, 32, 35

Moralists, 30–31, 128
  and moral philosophy, 103
  and practically practical knowledge, 87
Murphy, Arthur E., 111
Mystery
  and social science, 115
  in ethics and science, 34–35, 96

Natural law, 124, 143
  and affective connaturality, 33
  and Christian ethics, 90
  and Pascal, 146
  and religion, xi, 151
Nature, Philosophy of
  and modern science, 143
Newton, Isaac, 73, 154
Nietzsche, Friedrich
  and Socrates, 42, 112–13
  as moralist, 87, 104, 108

Original Sin, 145

Pascal, Blaise, 33, 73, 105
  as Jansenist, 144
  as moralist, 87, 104, 108
Peirce, Charles Sanders, 38n8
Phelan, Gerald B., 110
*Phronesis*
  see Practical wisdom
Plato, 42, 48, 62, 91, 120, 154
Political prudence, 94
Poverty, xi, 155
Practical truth
  and theoretical truth, 84
Practical wisdom, vii–ix, xii
  and art, 21
  and explanation, 81, 98
  and practically practical knowledge, 101
  and the singular, 31
  and uncertainty, 12, 15
  and virtue, 11, 21
Practically practical knowledge, 100–105, 107, 109–11

and science, x, 85–86
characterized, 80–82
Pre-Socratics, 137
Progress, 142–47
Prudence
see Practical wisdom
*Prudentia*
see Practical wisdom
Psychology, x, 140
Its relationship to moral philosophy, 47–51, 58
Ptolemy, 73
Pythagoreans, 91

Racine, Jean Baptiste, 87, 104
Russell, Bertrand, 105

Saint-Simon, Henri, 137–38
Sartre, Jean-Paul, 6
Shakespeare, William, 87, 104, 153
Social engineering, 120
Social science, viii
and the moralists, 128
and natural science, x, 7, 30, 116, 119, 138
and philosophy, 128, 132
as value free, xi, 61, 121, 126, 144
and virtue, 22
Socrates
and explanation, 35, 72
and fulfillment, 112–13
and moral science, 28, 42, 43ff.
and virtue, 30, 33
Sorel, Georges, 39$n$16, 112
Stoicism and the Stoics, 22, 120
Strauss, Leo, 134–36$n$13
Swift, Jonathan, 87, 104

Technical culture, 140
and humanism, 153–54
and misanthropy, 142
*see also* art
Thales, 116

Theology
　Moral, x, 106
　Unity of, 86, 103
Tolstoy, Leo, 38*n*5
Tradition, 97, 105

Ultimate practical judgment
　*see* Command
Use, 51–55, 57–61, 66
　and command, 20
　and moral philosophy, x, 100, 106
　and social science, xi

Values, 122, 128, 131
Virtue
　and science, 22
　Intellectual, 11, 110, 112
　Interconnection of, 21–22, 91
　Moral, ix, x, 10, 91
Volition
　Twelve phases of, 61

Weber, Max, 121, 123